INTRODUCTION TO MICROBIOLOGY

A Text book for graduate and post-graduate students of Indian Universities

Dr. Ranjan Kumar Sahoo, Ph.D
Associate Professor
Department of Biotechnology
Centurion University of Technology and Management
Bhubaneswar, Odisha, India.

Preface

The aim in presenting this book to the undergraduate and postgraduate students of various Indian universities is to provide them with an accurate and understandable matter on Microbiology. This book has been written as a text book for B.Sc. /B. Tech and M. Sc. /M. Tech and Pharmacy students.

The field of Microbiology is very wide and very vast research work has been done and still to be done. In the limited space and good standard, I have tried my best to incorporate all the principles and techniques which are mentioned in the syllabus of Indian Universities.

The author likes to acknowledge the support from Publisher, President, Vice-president, Vice-chancellor, Director and Dean of Centurion University of Technology and Management for their support and help. Lastly author dedicates this book to his mother, Late Sashirekha Sahoo, who was a teacher and influenced author to focus on publications.

I shall welcome and appreciate the suggestions for the further improvement of the book.

Ranjan Kumar Sahoo

Contents

Introduction to Microbiology

Microbiology is the branch of biology that deals with the study of small organisms that can be seen only under the microscope. Such organisms are called microorganisms, and are believed to be the primitive forms of life. They include many organisms like bacteria, virus, fungi etc.

Antonie Philips van Leeuwenhoek- Father of Microscopy

The development of microbiology begins from the invention of the microscope by Antonie van Leeuwenhoek and the implementation of his scientific method. His research opened up an entire world of microscopic life to the awareness of the scientists. It was he who first described bacteria, free-living and parasitic microscopic protists, sperm cells, blood cells, microscopic nematodes.

**Antonie van Leeuwenhoek
(1632-1723)**

Louis Pasteur: Father of Microbiology

Pasteur began his career as a chemist. He described the scientific basis for fermentation and wine making. He challenged the widely accepted myth of spontaneous generation, by using the swan neck experiment, there by setting the stage of modern biology. Pasteurs intuited that if germs were the cause of fermentation, they could just as well be the cause of contagious diseases. This proved to be true for many diseases such as potato blight, silkworm diseases and anthrax. Pasteur's work gave birth to many branch of science, and he was single handedly responsible for some of the most important theoretical concepts and practical applications of modern science.

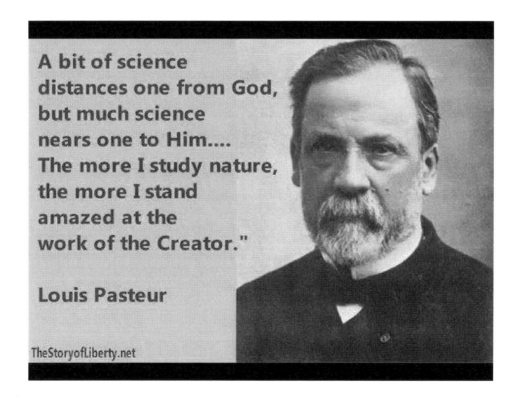

Louis Pasteur (December 27, 1822 – September 28, 1895)

Robert Koch and his postulates

Robert Koch who lived in Germany brought a new order to medicine and the study of disease. He lived at a time when people were deeply superstitious and attributed diseases to punishments from God or other strange occurrences in the universe. A staunch supporter of germ theory, Koch set-forth certain criteria for ascertaining the microbial causes to specific diseases. According to these postulates

1. The microbe must be present in every case of the disease.

2. The microbe must be isolated from the diseased "host" and grown in pure culture.

3. The disease must be reproduced when the pure culture is introduced to a non-diseased susceptible host.

4. The microbe must be recoverable from an experimentally infected host.

These postulates popularly known as **Koch's Postulates**

According him microbes can be identified with specific disease has helped people to find the cause and hopefully the cure too many diseases.

In 1882 he discovered the *Mycobacterium tuberculosis* as the cause of tuberculosis. He went on to lead an expedition in 1883 to India and Egypt and discovered the causative agent of Cholera- *Vibrio cholera*. Koch became the first to grow bacteria in colonies, first on potato slices and later on solid gelatine media. He was the first to use agar to solidify culture media.

Robert Koch (11 December 1843- 27 May 1910)

Joseph Lister- Father of Antiseptic Surgery

Sir Joseph Lister, Bt., was a British surgeon and a pioneer of antiseptic surgery. He promoted the idea of sterile surgery while working at the Glasgow Royal Infirmary. After having read about the work done by Louis Pasteur, Lister believed that it was microbes that were responsible for diseases to be spread in wards of hospitals. People who had been operated on were especially vulnerable as their bodies were weak and their skin had been cut open so that germs could gain entry into their body more easily. Lister covered the wound with lint soaked in carbolic acid. His success rate for patient survival was very high. He then devised a machine that pumped out a fine mist of carbolic acid into the air around during an operation. By doing so he found that the number of patients who died after his operation fell dramatically. For this reason, he is known as the '**Father of Antiseptic Surgery**.'

Joseph Lister (5 April 1827 – 10 February 1912)

Branches of Microbiology

Bacteriology: Deals with the study of bacteria

Mycology: Deals with the study of fungi

Parasitology: Study of protozoa and parasitic worms.

Virology: Deals with the study of viruses.

Applied areas of Microbiology

Technological advances have resulted in the development of major sub-disciplines of microbiology. These are

Agricultural microbiology: Deals with microbes associated with plant, plant and animal diseases, soil fertility, such as microbial degradation of organic matter and soil nutrient transformations.

Aquatic microbiology: Deals with the microorganisms living in an aquatic environment, that is, in the fresh water, salt water of a sea or ocean or the brackish water of a coastal estuary.

Industrial microbiology: Deals with the microbes which can be applied to create industrial products in mass quantities. There are multiple ways to manipulate a microorganism in order to increase maximum product yields.

Medical microbiology: It is a branch of medical science concerned with the prevention, diagnosis and treatment of infectious diseases. In addition, this field studies various clinical applications of microbes for the improvement of health.

Space microbiology: It is the study of microorganisms in outer space.

Environmental microbiology: Environmental microbiology is the study of microbial processes in the environment, microbial communities and microbial interactions.

Beneficial and Harmful effects of Microorganisms

Beneficial effects

1. Microbes are very important in food and beverage industries

2. They are integral components in our environment that aid in nutrient cycling.

3. Required for antibiotic production

4. Best tools in the study of genetic manipulations and treated as vital components in biotechnology.

5. Prevents the entry of pathogenic bacteria by covered human body as normal flora.

Harmful effects

1. They cause infectious diseases.

2. Normal flora sometimes act as pathogenic when change their position.

Microscopy

A microscope is a tool or machine with the ability to increase the visual size of an objec t , making it easier to observe. Microbiology is usually concerned with organisms so small that they cannot be seen directly with the unaided eye. A microscope is very important for the study of microorganisms.

All types of microscopes must perform two important functions.

a) They must magnify the specimen to a size that can be seen with the human eye.

b) They must provide a clear image that will enable microscopist to distinguish the component part of the specimen and this feature is called resolution. These may be accomplished by using visible light, ultraviolet light or electron beams.

Working principle of a microscope

A microscope produces an enlarged image of an object, this enlarged is known as its magnification. A magnified image of the object is first produced by one lens and then this image is further enlarged by a second lens to give a still more highly magnified image. The first lens, which is near the object, is called the objective, while the second lens, which is near the eye, is known as the eyepiece lens.

Magnification:

The total magnification of a microscope is the magnification of its objective by that of its eyepiece.

Magnifying power = $\dfrac{\text{Size of the image produced by the microscope}}{\text{Size of the image produced by unaided eye}}$

Resolving power

Ability of an instrument (microscope) or eye to distinguish two closely related points separately and distinctly is known as its **resolving power.** This is also defined as the limit of resolution and it is denoted as D. Resolving power depends on two factors, They are:

a) Wave length (λ) of light rays used.

b) Angle between the light access i.e. Numerical Aperature (NA).

A human eye has a resolving power of about 0.1 mm.

Numerical Aperture

It is the mathematical constant that describes the relative efficiency of a lens in bending light rays. It is denoted as (θ) and is defined as half the angle of the cone of light entering an objective.

Based on the type of light sources used there are different types of microscopes. They are;

(a) Light microscopes - it uses artificial light or sunlight for working. Example;
  (i) Bright Field Microscope
  (ii) Phase contrast microscope
  (iii) Dark field microscope
(b) Electron microscope- it uses a beam of electrons for illumination.
  (i) Scanning Electron Microscope
  (ii) Transmission Electron Microscope
  (iii) High voltage Electron Microscope

Bright Field Microscope

It is called Bright Field Microscope because it produces or forms a dark image against a bright background. It is used for ail laboratory and scientific work. Two types of Bright Field Microscopes are the simple microscope and compound microscopes. Simple microscopes are those containing single lens held in a frame like device. The effectiveness of the simple microscope is restricted because of its limited magnification, crude construction and other disadvantages. The compound microscope has wide spread applications in microbiology, associated branches of science and variety of industries. The compound microscope consists of a series of optical lenses, mechanical adjustment paths and supportive structures for its various components.

Compound Microscope and its Function

The mechanical parts of the microscope are concerned with support and adjustment of the optical path, whose function is to make an enlarged image of the object which we see. The following parts of microscope are

i) Base, Pillar and Inclination joint

The base of a microscope is horseshoe shaped or U-Shaped. Both the base and pillar serve to support the entire instrument. They are made heavy in order to minimize the vibration. The inclination joint permits the microscope to be tipped back to any degree desired by the observer.

ii) Arm and Body Tube

The arm supports the body tube to which the principle lenses are attached.

iii) Draw tube, Resolving nose piece, Tube length

The drawtube adjusts the tube length, which is the distance between the top lens of the ocular and the objective in the revolving nosepiece below. The system of lenses in the objective and oculars is made to function when ocular and objective are at a definite distance apart, which is called definite tube length. The drawtube is usually marked with a millimeter scale. A line running completely around the drawtube indicates the drawtube length in many microscopes. The rotating nose piece holds the objective lenses. It holds 3 types of objective lens: a) Low power b) High power c) Oil immersion. Objective lens collects the light rays from the object and produces the image with the eyepiece. It is the most important part of a microscope because the quality of the microscope depends on the magnification of the image produced by it. The major objective types in use are achromatic, apochromatic and fluorite.

The primary function of the objective includes;
(a) Gathering or concentrating the light ray coming from the specimen being viewed.
(b) Forming the image of the specimen.
(c) Magnifying the image.

Several important properties of microscopes are directly associated with the objectives. One of this is the resolving power or resolution. This feature is dependent on the wavelength of the light sources. The resolution is affected by the refractive index of the medium through which light passes before entering the microscope objective.

There are three different types of magnification power for different objectives. Low power objective has 10X magnification, high power objective has 40X magnification and oil immersion objective has a 100X magnification.

iv) Low Power Objective:

This objective is useful for the examination of protozoa and other large microorganisms. It can be used to study the colonies of growing organisms but individual bacteria can scarcely be made out with this lens. The Low power objective is usually much shorter, and has larger lens at its end. The low power is often marked "3" or "2/3" or "16 mm".

v) High Power Objective

This objective is used in microbiology for the examination of living microorganisms suspended in drops of water or other fluid. The high power objective is longer and more slender than the low power objective and the visible lens at its end is smaller than that of the low power.

vi) Oil Immersion Objective

This type of objective is used for the examination of stained smears of bacteria. The objective may be short or long , but it will always have a very small lens visible at the end. It is usually marked as "oil immer" or "llomogimmer". Equivalent focal length on the object-tives refers to the distance between the end of the objective and the object when in focus.

vii) Course and fine adjustment

The entire body of a microscope with its attached lenses is moved up and down by means of the rack and pinion of the course adjustment. The purpose of these adjustments is to bring the object into focus so that its outlines are sharp and clear. Both the fine and coarse adjustments are manipulated carefully, for it is a delicate machine.

viii) Stage

This is the part of the microscope on which the object to be examined is placed. The object is a transparent smear or any other preparation on a glass slide.

ix) Mirror

There are two types of reflecting mirrors in the light microscope. They are:

(a) Concave lens: To reflect artificial light source

(b) Plane mirror: To reflect natural light source

The mirror collects and reflects light up into the microscope. One side of the mirror is a plane mirror; and the other is a concave mirror. In most of the bacteriological work the concave mirror is used to concentrate the light

x) Sub stage condenser and diaphragm

Before the light reaches the object on the stage, it is condensed and focused by passage through the large condensing lens commonly called the 'Abbe condenser', in the sub stage. Condenser lens will collect light rays from the mirror and focuses in the form of a cone of light, i.e. converge to one point. The condenser is usually focused by rotating a knob to one side; the result is that maximum amount of light is directed upon the object.

xi) Iris diaphragm

Adjusts the amount of light passing into the condenser. The iris diaphragm consists of a number of leaves, which can be opened and closed by moving a small projecting lever.

xii) Eye piece lens

Magnifies the image produced by the objective and is available in many magnifications like 1x, 5x, 10x and 15x. Magnification of the object is equal to magnification power of the eye piece multiplied by Magnification of the objective.

Example: 10x X 100x =1000x

Working distance of a Microscope

Length of the Body tube =160 mm

Distance between specimen and objective lens is the focal length

Low power objective:

Focal length = Body tube length / Magnifying power Therefore 160 mm/10 =16 mm

High-Power objective:

Focal length =160mm/ 40x= 4mm

Oil immersion objective:

Focal length =160 /100x=1 .6mm.

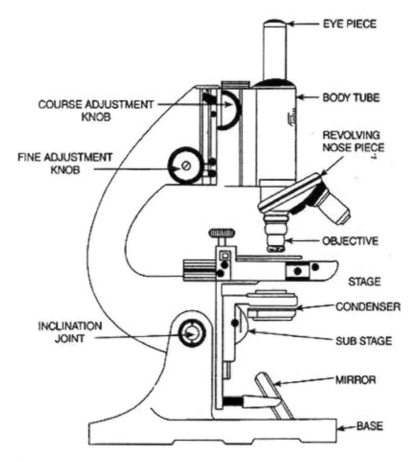

Figure: Different parts of a compound Microscope.

Use of the Microscope

Use of the microscope is acquired by practice. Certain steps should be taken into consideration while using a microscope. They are:

a) Clean the microscope before use.

b) Place the microscope near a source of light.

c) Place the object on the stage, swing into place the objective you wish to use, and while watching from the side, lower it to a point just under the position it will have when in focus.

d) Secure proper amount of light by manipulating the mirror, sub stage, condenser and the diaphragm.

e)   Focus first with the coarse , then with the fine adjustment until the object is clearly visible.

f)   Maintain the focus by continual manipulation of the fine adjustment.

Care of the Microscope

The microscope should be kept in its box when not in use. If it is in fairly constant service, it must be protected during intervals of work, from dust and also from strong light. This can be done by wrapping around it a clean duster, large enough to protect the condenser and the mirror. After use, oil should be wiped off the immersion lens, which is cleaned with a drop of xylol, and dried with a lens tissue, silk cloth, or soft handkerchief. While cleaning the oculars, objectives or the surface of the sub stage condenser, it is advisable not to rub them in a circular manner but wipe across them. It is essential that the cloth should be clean and free from particles of grit. Alcohol must not be used for cleaning lenses as it dissolves the cement in which they are set.

Dark Field Microscope

Principle

In this microscope the object is brightly illuminated against a dark background. This is accomplished by equipping the light microscope with a special kind of condenser that transmits a hollow cone of light from the source of illumination. The hollow cone of light is focused on the specimen (object) in such a way that unreflected and unrefracted rays do not enter the objective. This is the principle behind the working of a dark background microscope.

In the dark field microscope, a special condenser fits into the sub-stage in place of the ordinary condenser. The center of the top lens of this special condenser is opaque, so that none of the central rays of light can pass through it, and the object is illuminated only with oblique rays. None of the light goes directly up the objective as in the ordinary way, but instead the light rays pass through the object almost at right angles to the objective and nearly parallel to the stage.

Through the microscope, the field appears dark, but microorganisms or other objects in the preparation stand out sharply as very bright retractile bodies; just as the dust particles that appear in a beam of light across the cellar. The object has the property of self-luminescence. Since the light does not reach the objective, the only light that passes through the objective is the self-luminescent light produced by the object and the reflected light from the surroundings.

Use of the dark Field Microscope

a) The dark field microscope is used for the examination of unstained microorganisms or other objects suspended in fluids.

b) It is especially useful for the study of very small and delicate organisms, such as spirochete, which are invisible when viewed in the ordinary way.

c) It is also used to visualize internal structures in larger eukaryotic microorganisms.

d) Used to demonstrate the motility of bacteria.

Fluorescence Microscope

Fluorescent microscopes are used to provide structural details and other properties of a wide range of specimens. Such materials differ in their fluorescing power from their surroundings. This property of fluorescence is noted when substances become luminous upon their exposure to ultra violet rays. When certain substances including some dyes, fat, oil droplets are exposed to this form of radiation, they absorb energy of the invisible ultra violet light waves and emit it in the form of visible light waves.

Substances that exhibit fluorescence are called **Fluorochromes** or **fluorescent dyes.** This includes dyes like Acridine orange R, Auramine-O, Rhodamine, Isothiocyanide, Primulin, and Thiazo-yellow-G. These substances possess a particular selective action for microorganisms and their contents. In case of *Mycobacterium tuberculosis* it uses the dye Acridine orange, the bright yellow organism against a dark background indicates the presence of tubercle bacilli. Fluorescent microscopes require certain specific filter systems, along with objectives, condenser, and a suitable source of illumination. A special non-fluorescent type of immersion oil or glycerine is used to view the stained smears.

Parts of a Fluorescent Microscope

i) Mercury vapour lamp

It produces an ample supply of shorter wavelength of light that are needed for good fluorescence. The wavelength produced by the lamp includes the UV range of 200 nm- 400 nm, the wide range of 400 nm - 730 nm and the long infrared rays that are above 780nm.

ii) Filters

Excitation filter

It is placed next to the light source. When light is passed, it absorbs all the wave length of light and allows only light of longer wave length to pass through it, which is converted to shorter wave length that are required to excite the fluorochromes on the slide.

Barrier filter

It is placed next to the objective in between the objective and the eyepiece and it absorbs all light from the object and emits light of shorter wavelength to remove all remnants of the exciting light, so that only the fluorescence is seen.

iii) Condenser

A dark field condenser is used, which produces a better contrast, in a dark background. Another important feature is that the UV rays produced are deflected by the condenser, thus protecting the observers eye. The numerical aperture of the objective is always less than that of the condenser.

Working Principle

Light source is a heated mercury vapour lamp. The light emitted by the mercury vapour lamp falls on a reflecting mirror kept before the light source. This reflecting mirror collects all light and reflects light into the objective. All light rays then pass through an excitation filter, which then emits only a certain wavelength of light rays to fall on the object.

The deflected rays are then passed through a dark ground condenser which produces a dark back ground and thus provides better contrast. The excited rays then strike the fluorescent dye stained specimen on the slide and then pass through the objective lens, which reaches the barrier filter. The barrier filter then removes any remaining exciter wavelength light and finally emits light of a shorter wavelength, which are then passed to the eyepiece to get a better contrast image of the object.

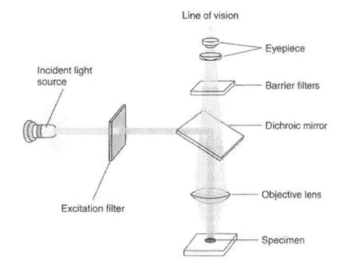

Figure: Optical diagram of fluorescence microscope.

Phase Contrast Microscopy

The phase contrast microscope is useful for visualizing cells or organisms because it permits viewing of cellular structures without the necessity of staining. This microscope helps to differentiate transparent protoplasmic structures without staining and killing them. It was developed by Frederick Zernike in 1933 and is also called Zernike Microscope. It is used for studying living protozoa and transparent cells.

Working Principle

It works on the principle of phase difference produced by the cells. Each cellular component in cells has different thickness and each have different refractive index and hence light frequency will vary in each component. This variation is called phase difference, which will finally make a dark image or a bright image.

Parts of the Phase Contrast Microscope

Along with the usual parts of the microscope, the phase contrast microscope has certain other parts like:

i) Annular diaphragm

It consists of an annular stop that allows only a hollow cone of light rays to pass up through the condenser to the object on the slide. It is placed next to the condenser and helps to produce a clear cone of light.

ii) Annular phase plate

It is a special optical disk located next to the objective lens. It collects two types of waves from the objective and has two grooves. It has a phase ring that advances or retards the direct light rays to one fourth of its wavelength.The direct rays converge on the phase ring to be advanced or retarded one-fourth the wavelength. These rays emerge as solid lines from the object on the slide. This ring on the phase plate is coated with a material that will produce the desired phase shift.

The diffracted rays, which have already been retarded one fourth the wavelength miss the phase ring and are not affected by the phase plate. It should be clear that depending on the type of phase contrast microscope, the convergence of diffracted and direct rays on the image plane would result in either a bright image or darker image. The former is referred to as bright phase microscopy and the later is known as dark phase microscopy.

The image obtained in phase contrast microscope is four times bright or dark as seen through the bright field microscope. Thus with a phase contrast microscope, living organisms can be clearly observed in great detail without staining them, permitting the study of their movement in the medium in which they are growing. It is used to observe and study the movement of chromosomes and other cellular events during the mitosis and meiosis stages of cell division.

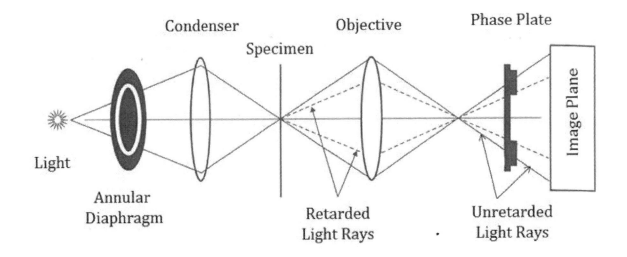

Figure: Optics of the phase contrast microscope

17

Electron Microscope

An Electron Microscope differs markedly in many respects from the optical microscopes. This technique has both strengths and weaknesses. In electron microscopy, resolution is much better, but specimen preparation and instrument operation are often more difficult. In electron microscope the specimen to be examined is prepared as an extremely thin dry film on small screens and is introduced into the instrument at a point between the magnetic condenser and the magnetic objective. The magnified image is viewed on a fluorescent screen through an airtight window or recorded on a photographic plate by a camera built into the instrument. It is used for studying the detailed internal structure of microorganisms.

Electron Microscopes are made in two basic designs: Transmission Electron Microscope (TEM) and Scanning Electron Microscope (SEM). Another two types the Scanning Transmission Electron Microscope, and High Voltage Electron Microscopy (HVEM) is the modification of electron microscopes. Both scanning and transmission electron microscopes are similar in that each uses a beam of electrons to produce an image. These instruments use quite different mechanisms to form the final image.

Transmission Electron Microscope

Most parts of the transmission electron microscope are similar to the light microscope. It has a resolution 10,000 times better than the light microscope and points closer than 5 angstrom/5nm can be easily distinguished. It is very complex and sophisticated.

Parts of the Transmission Electron Microscope (TEM)

It includes parts like vacuum system, electron gun, electromagnetic lenses and photographic system.

i) Vacuum system

Electrons cannot travel very far in air; a strong vacuum must be maintained along the entire path of the electron beam. Two types of vacuum pumps work together to create vacuum in the column of an electron microscope. A standard rotary pump is used to achieve the initial low vacuum when the instrument is first started up. The oil diffusion pump achieves the high vacuum required for operation. The diffusion pump is oil filled reservoir in which oil is vaporized by heating. As the oil vapour rises it traps air molecules and is then condensed by condensing vanes, which are cooled by circulating cold water. The diffusion pump cannot function independently, it requires back up by the rotary pump to remove the trapped air molecules by the system. In some TEMs, a device called a cold finger is incorporated into the vacuum system to help establish a high vacuum. The cold finger is a metal insert in the column of the microscope that is cooled by liquid nitrogen. The cold finger attracts gases and random contaminating molecules, which then solidify on the cold metal surface.

ii) Electron gun

The electron beam in a TEM is generated by an electron gun, an assembly of several components. The cathode, a tungsten filament similar to a light bulb filament, emits electrons from the surface when it is heated. The cathode tip is near a circular opening in a metal housing called the Wehnelt cylinder. A negative voltage on the cylinder helps to control electron emission and shape the beam. At the other end of the cylinder is the anode. The anode is kept at 0 V, while the cathode is maintained at 50 -100 kV. This difference in voltage is called the accelerating voltage because it causes the electrons to accelerate as they pass through the cylinder.

ii) Electromagnetic lenses

The formation of an image using electron microscopy depends on both the wave like and the particle like properties of electrons. The electromagnetic lenses control the beams of electrons that are produced. Since the electrons are charged, they are subject to magnetic forces when the move. The principle can be used to change the direction of the electromagnetic beam. As the electron beam leaves the upper region of me condenser lens system, it enters a series of lenses made of electromagnets. The lens itself is simply a space influenced by an electromagnetic field. The focal length of each lens can be increased or decreased by varying the current applied to its energizing coils. When several lenses are arranged, they can control illumination, focus and magnification.

The condenser lens is the first lens to affect the electron beam. It functions in the same fashion as its counterpart in the light microscope to focus the beam on the specimen. Most electron microscopes actually use a condenser lens system with two lenses to achieve better focus of the electron beam. The next component is the objective lens, which is the most important part of the microscope. The specimen is positioned on the specimen stage with the objective lens. The objective lens, which is in contact with the intermediate lens and the projector lens, produces a final image on a viewing screen of zinc sulphide that fluoresces when struck by the electron beam.

The electron beam generated by the cathode passes through the condenser lens system and impinges on the specimen. As the beam strikes the specimen, some electrons are scattered by the sample, where as others continue in their paths relatively unimpeded. The scattering of electrons is the result of properties created in the specimen by the preparation procedure. Specimen preparation imparts selective electron density to the specimen, i.e., some areas become more opaque to electrons than others. Such electron dense areas of the specimen will appear dark because few electrons pass through, whereas others will appear lighter because they permit the passage of more electrons. The contrasting light, dark and intermediate areas of the specimen create the image seen on the screen. The fact that the image is formed by differing extents of electron transmission through the specimen is reflected in the term Transmission Electron Microscope.

Photographic system

The image obtained by electron microscopy can be recorded photographically as an electron micrograph, which then becomes a permanent photographic record of the specimen. Most transmission electron microscopes have a camera chamber mounted directly beneath the viewing screen. The camera is a little more than a box that allows photographic plates to be moved manually or automatic ally to the area immediately beneath the viewing screen.

To photograph a specimen, the microscopist simply aligns the image on the screen, focuses the image with the objective lens control, adjusts the illumination to a predetermined intensity with the condenser adjustment and makes the exposure. The exposure may be made automatically or by lifting the screen with a lever on the microscope console. Once the exposure is made, the plate is advanced out of the exposure position to a container where it is stored until retrieved from the instrument for later development and printing.

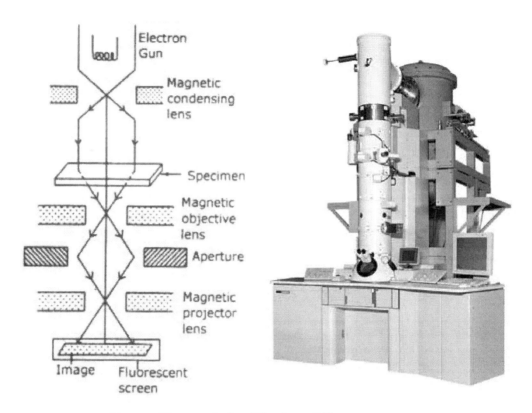

Figure: Transmission Electron Microscope

Scanning Electron Microscope

Scanning electron Microscopy is a type of electron microscopy which generates an image by scanning the specimen with a beam of electrons. The vacuum system and electron source are similar to those found in the transmission electron microscope, although the accelerating voltage is much lower (about 5 - 30 kV). The significant difference between the two kinds of instruments lies in the way the image is formed. In the SEM, a magnetic lens system focuses the beam of electrons into an intense spot on the surface of the specimen. The spot is moved back and forth across the specimen by charged plates called **beam deflectors** located between the condenser lens and the specimen.

The beam def lectors attract or repel the beam according to the signals sent to them by the deflector circuitry. As the electron beam sweeps rapidly over the specimen, molecules in the specimen are excited to high energy levels and emit **secondary electrons.** These secondary electrons are used to form an image of the specimen surface. They are then captured by a detector that is located immediately above and to one side of the specimen. The essential component of the detector is a **scintillator,** which emits photons of light when excited by the electron incident upon it. The photons are then used to generate an electronic signal to a video screen. The image then develops point-by-point, line-by-line on the screen as the primary electron beam sweeps over the specimen.

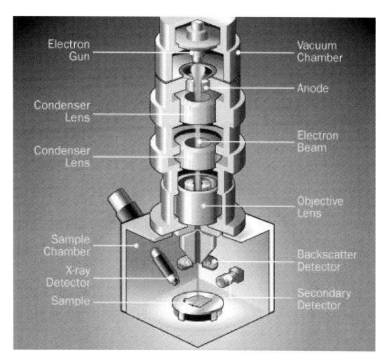

Figure: Scanning Electron Microscope

Scanning Transmission Electron Microscopy

Scanning Transmission Electron Microscopy (STEM) contains elements of both transmission and scanning electron microscopes. It also uses an electron beam that sweeps over the specimen. But the image is then formed by electrons transmitted through the specimen, as with TEM. A STEM is capable of distinguishing specific characteristics of the electrons that are transmitted by the specimen, thus deriving information about the specimen not obtainable with a conventional TEM. Scanning Transmission Electron Microscope is technically sophisticated, requires a very high vacuum, and is much more electronically complex than a Transmission Electron Microscope or a Scanning Electron Microscope.

High Voltage Electron Microscopy

A high voltage electron microscope (HVEM) is very similar to transmission electron microscope only its accelerating voltage is much higher. HVEM uses voltage of about 200 to 1000 kV, but TEM uses accelerating voltage of 50 to 100 kV. Due to the high voltage and greatly reduced chromatic aberration relatively thick specimens can be examined with good

22

resolution. Cellular structures can be studied in sections as thick as 1μm, about 10 times thicker than the ordinary TEM.

Sample Preparation Techniques for electron microscope

Specimen for electron microscopy is prepared in different ways depending on the type of microscope and kind of information the microscopist wants to obtain. The methods used are very complicated, time consuming and costly compared to the methods of light microscopy. Living specimens cannot be examined because the vacuum to which the specimens are exposed in an electron microscope will kill the organism. Sample preparation methods include fixation, negative staining, shadowing, freeze fracturing, freeze etching etc .

Short notes

1. Microscopes are optical instruments that magnify objects with the help of lenses.

2. Based on the type of light sources used there are different types of microscopes. They are

    a) Light microscopes - it uses artificial light or sunlight for working.
        Example   i) Bright Field Microscope
                        ii) Phase Contrast Microscope
                        iii) Dark Field Microscope
    b) Electron microscopes- it uses a beam of electrons for illumination.
        Example   i) Scanning Electron Microscope
                        ii) Transmission Electron Microscope.

3. The compound Microscope has the following parts: They are base, pillar, and inclination joint, arm, rotating nosepiece, which holds the objective lenses. It holds 3 types of objective lenses. They are low power, high power, and oil immersion lenses.

4. Fluorescent microscopes are used to provide a means of studying the structural details and other properties of a wider range of specimens. Two filters are present in fluorescent microscopes, which specifically passes the light through them, they are excitation filter and barrier filters.

5. The phase contrast microscope is useful for visualizing cells or organisms because it permits viewing of cellular structures without the necessity of staining. This microscope helps to differentiate transparent protoplasmic structures without staining and killing them. It is used for studying living protozoa and transparent cells. It works on the principle of phase difference produced by the cells.

6. In electron microscopy, resolution is much better, but specimen preparation and instrument operation are often more difficult. The magnified image is viewed on a fluorescent screen through an airtight window or recorded on a photographic plate by a camera built into the instrument. It is used for studying the detailed internal structure of microorganisms.

7. Electron Microscope is made in two basic designs: the Transmission Electron Microscope (TEM) and Scanning Electron Microscope (SEM). A third type of instrument, the Scanning Transmission Electron Microscope (STEM), is a hybrid of the two electron Microscopes. Both scanning and Transmission Electron Microscopes are similar in that each uses a beam of electrons to produce an image.

Units of measurement in microscopy

Unit	Symbol	Value	Object type
1 Meter	m		
1 Centimeter	cm	$10 \text{ mm} = 10^{-2}$ meter	
1 Millimeter	mm	$1000\mu = 10^{-3}$ meter	Giant cells, eggs, protozoans
1 Micrometer / Micron	μm	$1000 \text{ m}\mu = 10^{-6}$ meter	Cell organelles, bacteria
1 Nanometer/ Millimicron	nm / mμ	10^{-9} meter	Viruses, macromolecules
1 Angstrom	Å	10^{-10} meter	Molecules

Microbial Taxonomy

Introduction

The microbial world has an extra ordinary diversity in their morphology, physiology, genetics etc, because of the bewildering diversity of microbes. It is essential to classify them into groups based on their mutual similarities, until the last century living organisms were classified as plants or animals based on their visual difference in form and constitution. These were later accepted as two broad kingdoms of living creatures. This classification was made before the discovery of microorganisms. During the course of studies it became evident that the old and common divisions of living world were insufficient because some microorganisms showed similarity with plants. Bacteria were first included under plants. Slime molds were regarded as a middle path between plants and animals, because they were considered as plants by botanists and animals by zoologists, thus they created a new kingdom.

The new kingdom was called Protista. The kingdom includes all those microorganisms, which do not possess any extensive development of tissue. The kingdom Protista contains those organisms that are differentiated from plants and animals by their lack of morphological specialization, most of them being unicellular. The Protista can be further subdivided into two clearly differentiated groups on the basis of their cellular structure. The higher protests resemble plants and animals in their cell composition, so they are called **eukaryotes.** This group includes algae, fungi, and the protozoans. Viruses are non-cellular particles, they are included in the group **akaryota** different from all other organisms, in that they are not capable of self-replication and can proliferate only in living cells.

Lower Protists (Prokaryota)

Prokaryotic protists are those microorganisms, which lack distinct nucleus and plastids. These are sub divided into bacteria and Cyanobacteria (blue green algae). On the basis of the mechanism of movement and character of cell wall these organisms can be differentiated.

Taxonomy

Taxonomy is the science, which consists of three separate but interrelated parts; they are a) classification, b) nomenclature, c) identification.

a) Classification: it is the orderly arrangement of organisms into group or taxa, based on mutual similarity or evolutionary relatedness.

b) Nomenclature: it is the branch of taxonomy concerned with the assignment of names to taxonomic groups in agreement with published rules

c) Identification: it is the practical approach to taxonomy, and is the process of determining a particular isolate, which belongs to a recognized taxon.

Systematics

It is termed and defined as the scientific study of organisms with the ultimate object of characterizing and arranging them in an orderly manner. It includes disciplines like morphology, ecology, epidemiology, biochemistry, molecular biology and physiology. Though newer molecular techniques are being used in classifying microorganisms, which have generated new advances and excitement in microbial taxonomy, more approaches have to be made from it.

The taxonomic hierarchy

All organisms can be grouped into a series of subdivisions that make up the taxonomic hierarchy. Linnaeus developed this hierarchy for the classification of plants and animals. A genus consists of species that differ from each other in certain ways but are related by descent. Even though each species differs from every other species, they are all related genetically. Just as a number of species make up a genus, related genera make up a family. A group of similar families constitutes an order, and a group of similar orders makes up a class. Related classes, in turn make up a phylum. (In botany, the comparable term division has been used; it is equivalent to phylum). All phyla or divisions are related to each other and make up a kingdom.

For example, the scientific classification for the bacteria E. coli can be given as follows

Domain: Bacteria
Phylum: Proteobacteria
Class: Gamma Proteobacteria
Order: Enterobacterials
Family: Enterobacteriaceae
Genus: Escherichia
Species: E. coli

Informal names are often used in place of formal hierarchical ones. Typical examples of such names are purple bacteria, spirochetes, methane-oxidizing bacteria, sulphate reducing bacteria and lactic acid bacteria. The basic in microbial taxonomy is the species.

Species of bacteria

Bacterial species are characterized by phenotypic and genotypic differences. It is a collection of strains that share main stable properties and differ significantly from other groups of strains.

Strains

Strain is a population of organisms that descends from a single organism or pure culture isolate. Strains within a species may differ slightly from one another in many ways.

Biovars: they are variant bacterial strains that are characterized by biochemical or physiological differences.

Morphovars: they differ morphology

Serovars: they have distinctive antigenic properties.

Type strain

It is one strain of a species. It is usually one of the first strains studied and often is more fully characterized than other strains. It does not have to be the most representative member.

Genus

Every species is assigned to a genus and is the next rank in the taxonomic hierarchy. It is a well-defined group of one or more species and is clearly separate from other genera.

The study of phylogenetic relationships

In 2001 an international project called the all species Inventory was launched. The project's purpose is to identify and record every species of life on earth in the next 25 years. Among these many and diverse organisms, however, are many similarities. For example, all organisms are composed of cells surrounded by a plasma membrane, use ATP for energy, and store their genetic information in DNA. These similarities are the result of evolution, or descent from a common ancestor. In 1859, the English naturalist Charles Darwin proposed that natural selection was responsible for the similarities as well as the differences among organisms. The differences can be attributed to the survival of organisms with traits best suited to a particular environment.

To facilitate research, scholarship and communication, we arrange organisms into taxonomic categories, or taxa, to show degrees of similarities among organisms. These similarities are due to relatedness-all organisms are related through evolution. Systematics, or phylogeny, is the study of evolutionary history of organisms.

From the time of Aristotle, living organisms were categorized in just two ways, either plants or animals. In 1735, the Swedish botanist Carolus Linnaeus introduced a formal system of classification dividing organisms into two kingdoms-Plantae and Animalia. He used Latinized names to provide one common "language" for systematics.

With the advent of electron microscopy, the physical differences between cells became apparent. The term prokaryote was introduced in 1973 by Edward Chatton to distinguish cells having no nucleus from the nucleated cells of plants and animals. In 1961, Roger Stainer provided the current definition of prokaryotes: cells in which the nuclear material is not surrounded by a nuclear membrane. In 1968, Robert G.E. Murray proposed the Kingdom Prokaryota.

In 1969, Robert H. Whittaker founded the five kingdom system in which prokaryotes were placed in the Kingdom Prokaryotae, or Monera, and eukaryotes comprised the other four kingdoms. The Kingdom Prokaryotae had been based on microscopic observations. Subsequently, new techniques in molecular biology revealed that there are actually two types of prokaryotic cells and one type of eukaryotic cell.

The three domains

The discovery of three cell types was based on the observations that ribosomes are not the same in all cells. Ribosomes provide a method of comparing cells because ribosomes are present in all cells. Comparing the sequences of nucleotides in ribosomal RNA (rRNA) from different kinds of cells shows that there are distinctly different cell groups: the eukaryotes and two types of prokaryotes- the bacteria and the archaea.

In 1978, Carl R. Woese proposed elevating the three cell types to a level above kingdom, called domain. Woese believed that the archaea and the bacteria, although similar in appearance, should form their own separate domains on the evolutionary tree. In this widely accepted scheme, animals, plants, fungi and protists are kingdoms in the domain eukaryotes. Organisms are classified by cell type in the three domain systems. In addition to differences in rRNA, the three domains differ in membrane lipid structure, transfer RNA molecules and sensitivity to antibiotics.

The domain bacteria include all the pathogenic prokaryotes as well as many of the non-pathogenic prokaryotes found in soil and water. The photoautotrophic prokaryotes as well as many of the non-pathogenic prokaryotes are found in soil and water. The photoautotrophic prokaryotes are also in this domain. The domain archaea includes prokaryotes that do not have peptidogycan in their cell walls. They often live in extreme environments and carry out unusual processes. Archaea include three major groups:

1. **The methanogens,** strict anaerobes that produce methane from carbon dioxide and hydrogen.
2. **Extreme halophiler,** which require high concentrations of salt for survival.
3. **Hyperthermophiles,** which normally grow in hot environments.

The evolutionary relationship of the three domains is the subject of current research by biologists. Originally, archaea were thought to be the most primitive group, whereas bacteria were assumed to be more closely related to eukaryotes. However studies of rRNA indicate that a universal ancestor split into three lineages. That split led to the archaea, the bacteria and what eventually became the nucleoplasm of the eukaryotes. Eukaryotic cells evolved more recently, about 1.4 billion years ago. According to the endosymbiotic theory, eukaryotic cells evolved from prokaryotic cells living inside one another, as endosymbionts. In fact the similarities between prokaryotic cells and eukaryotic organelles provide striking evidence for this endosymbiotic relationship.

The original nucleoplasmic cell was prokaryotic. However, infolding in its plasma membrane may have surrounded the nuclear region to produce a true nucleus. The cell provided the original host in which endosymbiotic bacteria developed into organelles.

Taxonomy provides tools for clarifying the evolution of organisms, as well as their interrelationships. New organisms are being discovered every day, and taxonomists continue to search for a natural classification system that reflects phylogenetic relationships.

Classification system

A good classification should bring order to biological diversity and may even clarify the functions of a morphological structure. The best natural classification system may be a phonetic system, which group's organisms based on the mutual similarity of their phenotypic characters. Phenetic studies reveal possible evolutionary relationships; they are not dependent on phylogenetic analysis.

Natural classification

The most desirable classification system called natural classification based largely on anatomical characteristics, arranges organisms into groups whose members share many characteristics and reflects as much as possible the biological nature of the organism. Many taxonomists suggest that the most natural classification is one with greatest information content or predicted value.

Phyletic classification

The system of classification is based on the evolutionary relationship rather than general resemblance. This had proved difficult for bacteria and other microorganisms, because of lack of fossil record. The direct comparison of genetic material; and gene products such as RNA and proteins overcome some of these problems.

Numerical taxonomy

The development of computers made possible the quantitative approach known as numerical taxonomy. Peter H.A. Sneath and Robert Sokal defined numerical taxonomy as the grouping by the numerical methods of taxonomic units into taxa on the basis of their characteristics. This method has proved to be a very powerful tool in microbial taxonomy. Computers are used for numerical analysis to get information about the properties of the organism. The resulting classification is based on the general similarity judged by comparison of many characteristics by giving importance to it. This approach becomes feasible with computers because of the large number of calculations involved in it.

Some of the important aspects of numerical taxonomy are:

a) The process begins with a determination of the presence or absence of selected characters in the group of organisms under study.

b) A character usually is defined as an attribute about which a single statement can be made.

c) Many characters are compared for a accurate and reliable classification.

d) Many different kinds of data like morphological, biochemical, and physiological are included.

e) After character analysis, association coefficient is calculated for each organism in the pair.

f) The simple matching coefficient, which is the most commonly used coefficient in bacteriology, is the proportion of characters that match regardless of whether the attribute is absent or present.

g) The simple matching coefficient or other association coefficient are then arranged to form a similarity matrix. This is a matrix in which the rows and columns represent organisms and each value is an association coefficient measuring the similarity of two different organisms, so that each organism is compared to every other one in table.

h) Organisms with greater similarity are grouped together and separated from dissimilar organisms; such groups of organisms are called phenons.

i) The results of numerical taxonomic analysis are often summarized with a tree like diagram called a dendrogram.

Phenetic classification and Bergey's manual

In the past it was not that easy to classify bacteria based on phylogenetic relationships. The characteristics used to define sections are normally features such as general shape, and morphology, gram staining property, oxygen relationship, motility, presence of endospores, the mode of energy production, etc.

Scientific nomenclature

Every organism is assigned two names, or binomial name. These names are the genus name and specific epithet (species), and both names are printed underlined or italicized. The genus name is always capitalized and is always a noun. The species name is lowercase and is usually an adjective. Because this system gives two names to each organism, the system is called binomial nomenclature.

Let us consider some examples. Our own genus and specific epithet are Homo sapiens. The noun or genus means man; the adjective or specific epithet means wise. A mold that contaminates bread is called *Rhizopus nigricans*. Rhizo (root) describes root like structures on the fungus; Niger identifies the colour of its spore sacs. Scientists use binomials worldwide, regardless of their native language, which enables them to share knowledge efficiently and accurately. Several scientific entities are responsible for establishing rules governing the naming of organisms. Several scientific entities are responsible for establishing names for protozoa and parasitic worms and are published in the International Code of Zoological Nomenclature.

Methods of classifying and identifying microorganisms

A classification scheme provides a list of characteristics and a means for comparison to aid in the identification of an organism. Once an organism is identified, it can be placed into a previously devised classification scheme. Microorganisms are identified for practical purposes-for example, to determine an appropriate treatment for an infection. They are not necessarily identified by the same techniques by which they are classified. Following characteristics are used in classifying and identifying microorganisms:

Morphological characteristics

Morphological features are easy to study and analyze, particularly in eukaryotic microorganisms and are more complex in prokaryotes. Morphological comparison is important because structural features depend on the expression of many genes. They are usually genetically stable and normally do not vary greatly with environmental changes. Thus the morphological similarity is a good indication of phylogenetic relatedness, physiological and metabolic characteristics. These characteristics are directly related to the activity of microbial enzymes and transport proteins. Since proteins are gene products analysis of these characteristics provide an indirect composition of microbial genomes.

Ecological characteristics

Ecological characteristics also affect microorganisms, which has a taxonomic value. Sometimes very closely related microbes can differ considerably with respect to ecological characteristics. Microorganisms living in various parts of the human body markedly differ from one another and from those growing in fresh water, terrestrial and marine environments. Life cycle patterns, the nature of symbiotic relationships, the ability to cause disease in a particular host, and habitat preferences such as temperature, pH, oxygen and osmotic concentration are other examples of taxonomically important ecological properties.

Differential staining

One of the first steps in identifying bacteria is differential staining. Most bacteria are either gram-positive or gram-negative. Other differential stains, such as the acid-fast stain, can be useful for a more limited group of microorganisms. These stains are based on the chemical composition of cell walls and therefore are not useful in identifying either the wall-less bacteria or the archaea with unusual walls.

Biochemical tests

Enzymatic activities are widely used to differentiate bacteria. Even closely related bacteria can usually be separated into distinct species by subjecting them to ferment an assortment of selected carbohydrates. For example these biochemical tests are used to identify bacteria. Moreover, biochemical tests can provide insight into a species niche in the ecosystem. For example a bacterium that can fix nitrogen gas or oxidize elemental sulfur will provide important nutrients for plants and animals.

Phage typing

Phage typing is a test determining which phages of bacterium is susceptible to bacteriophages. They are highly specialized, in that they usually infect only members of a particular species, or even particular strains within a species. One bacterial strain may be susceptible to two different phages, whereas another strain of the same species might be susceptible to those two phages plus a third phage.

Fatty acid profiles

Bacteria synthesize a wide variety of fatty acids, and in general, these fatty acids are constant for a particular species. A commercial system has been designed to separate cellular fatty acids to compare them to fatty acids profile of known organisms. Fatty acid profiles often need to be backed up by biochemical testing and they can be used only for identification, not to determine phylogenetic relatedness.

Flow cytometry

It can be used to identify bacteria in a sample without culturing the bacteria and is forced through a small opening. The simplest method detects the presence of bacteria by detecting the difference in electrical conductivity between cells and the surrounding medium. If a laser illuminates the fluid passing through the opening, the scattering of light provides information about the cell size, shape, density and surface, which is analyzed by a computer.

Genetic analysis

Most of the eukaryotes are able to reproduce sexually; therefore the genetic analysis of microorganisms is considerably important in classifying them. Prokaryote do not reproduce sexually, therefore the study of chromosomal gene exchange, transformation and conjugation is important during their classification.

Molecular characteristics

Studies of protein and nucleic acids have recently been introduced as powerful approaches to taxonomy, because it directs gene products or the gene themselves for the comparison of protein and nucleic acid, which also yields useful information about the true relatedness.

Comparison of proteins

The amino acid sequences of proteins have direct reflections of mRNA sequence and therefore it is closely related to structures of the gene coding and their synthesis. Thus the comparison of proteins from different microorganisms is very useful taxonomically. The sequences of cytochromes and other electron transport proteins, histones and a variety of enzymes have been used in taxonomic studies. The electrophoretic mobility of proteins are also important in studying relationships at the species and sub species level.

Antigen- Antibody reactions *Invitro*

Antibodies can discriminate between very similar proteins. Immunologic techniques are used to compare proteins from different microorganisms.

Nucleic acid sequencing

Sequencing DNA and RNA can directly compare the genome structures. Techniques for rapidly sequencing both DNA and RNA are now available. RNA sequencing has been more extensively used in microbial taxonomy. The rRNA is most ideal for studies of microbial evolution and relatedness since they are essential to a critical organelle found in all microorganisms. Their functional role is the same as in all ribosomes. Ribosomal RNAs can be characterized in terms of partial sequences by the oligonucleotide cataloging method.

Ribosomal RNA sequencing

Ribosomal RNA (rRNA) sequencing is currently being used to determine the diversity of organisms and the phylogenetic relationships among them. There are several advantages to using rRNA. First all cells contain ribosomes. Two closely related organisms would have fewer different bases in their rRNA than two organisms that are distantly related. Another advantage is that RNA genes have undergone few changes over time. The rRNA used most often is a component of the smaller portion of ribosomes. A third advantage of rRNA sequencing is that cells do not have to be cultured in the laboratory.

DNA base composition

A classification technique that has come into wide use among taxonomists is the determination of an organisms DNA base composition. This base composition is usually expressed as the percentage of guanine plus cytosine (G+C).

The base composition of a single species is theoretically a fixed property; thus a comparison of the G+C content in different species can reveal the degree of species relatedness. Each guanine (G) in DNA has a complementary cytosine (C). Similarly, each adenine (A) in the DNA has a complementary thymine (T). Therefore the percentage of DNA bases that are GC pairs also tells us the percentage that are AT pairs (GC+AT=100%). Two organisms that are closely related and hence have many identical or similar genes will have similar amounts of the various bases in their DNA.

The base composition of DNA can be determined in several ways. Although the G+C content can be chemically ascertained after hydrolysis of DNA and separation of its bases, physical methods are easier and more often used. The G+C content is often determined from the melting temperature (Tm) of DNA.

DNA fingerprinting

Determining the entire sequence of bases in an organism DNA is now possible with modern biochemical methods, but this is currently impractical for laboratory identification because great amount of time required. The use of restriction enzymes enables researchers to compare the base sequences of different organisms. Restriction enzymes cut a molecule of DNA wherever a specific base sequence occurs producing restriction fragments.

In this technique, the DNA from two microorganisms is treated with the same restriction enzyme and the restriction fragments produced are separated by electrophoresis on a thin layer of agar. A comparison of the number and sizes of restriction fragments that are produced from different organisms provides information about their genetic similarities and differences; the more similar the patterns or DNA fingerprints, the more closely related are the organisms. DNA fingerprinting is used to determine the source of hospital acquired infections.

Nucleic acid hybridization

If a double stranded molecule of DNA is subjected to heat, the complementary strands will separate as the hydrogen bonds between the bases break. If the single strands are then cooled slowly, they will reunite to form a double stranded molecule identical to the original double strand. When this technique is applied to separate DNA strands from two different organisms, it is possible to determine the extent of similarity between the sequences of the two organisms. This method is known as nucleic acid hybridization.

The procedure assumes that if two species are similar or related, a major portion of their nucleic acid sequences will also be similar. The procedure measures the ability of DNA strands from one organism to hybridize with the DNA strands of another organism. The greater the degree of hybridization, the greater is the degree of relatedness. RNA is single stranded and is transcribed from one strand of DNA; a particular strand of RNA, therefore is complementary to the strand of DNA from which it was transcribed and will hybridize with that separated strand of DNA. DNA-RNA hybridization can thus be used to determine relatedness between DNA from one organism and RNA from another organism in the same way that DNA-DNA hybridization is used. Nucleic acid hybridization can be used to identify unknown microorganisms by Southern blotting. In addition, rapid identification methods using DNA probes are being developed. An exciting new technology is the DNA chip, which will make it possible to quickly detect a pathogen in a host by identifying a gene that is unique to that pathogen.

The DNA chip is composed of DNA probes. A sample containing DNA from an unknown organism is labeled with a fluorescent dye and added to the chip. Hybridization between the probe DNA and DNA in the sample is detected by fluorescence.

The Polymerase Chain Reaction (PCR)

When a microorganism cannot be cultured by conventional methods, the causative agent of an infectious disease might not be recognized. A technique called the Polymerase Chain Reaction (PCR) can be used to increase the amount of microbial DNA to levels that can be tested by gel electrophoresis.

Putting classification methods together

Morphological characteristics, differential staining, and biochemical testing were the only identification tools available just a few years ago. Technological advancements are making it possible to use nucleic acid analysis techniques, once reserved for classification for routine identification.

Information about microbes obtained by these methods is used to identify and classify the organisms. Two methods of using the information are described below.

a) Dichotomous keys

Dichotomous keys are widely used for identification. In a dichotomous key, identification is based on successive questions and each question has two possible answers. After answering one question, the investigator is directed to another question until an organism is identified. Although these keys often have little to do with phylogenetic relationships, they are invaluable for identification.

b) Cladograms (clado means branch)

Cladograms are maps that show evolutionary relationships among organisms. A feature shared by various species on the branch defines each branch point on the cladograms. Historically, cladograms for vertebrates were made using fossil evidence; however, rRNA sequences are now being used to confirm assumptions based on fossils. Most microorganisms do not leave fossils; therefore, rRNA sequencing is primarily used to make cladograms for microorganisms. The small rRNA subunit used has 1500 bases and computer programs do the calculations.

Short notes

> The microbial world has extra ordinary diversity in their morphology, physiology, genetics etc. because of the bewildering diversity of microbes; it is essential to classify them into groups based on their mutual similarities.

> Taxonomy is the science, which consists of three separate but interrelated parts; they are classification, nomenclature and identification.

> Systematics is termed and defined as the scientific study of organisms with the ultimate object in of characterizing and arranging them in an orderly manner. It includes disciplines like morphology, ecology, epidemiology, biochemistry, molecular biology and physiology. The most commonly used levels or ranks are species, genera, families, orders, classes, phyla or divisions and kingdoms.

> Taxonomists name biological organisms by using the binomial system introduced by Swedish botanist Carolus Linnaeus. The Latinized, italictized name consists of two parts: the first part which is capitalized and is the generic name. The second is the uncapitalized and is the species name. The specific name is stable. The generic name can change if the organism is assigned to another genus because of new information.

➢ Morphological characteristics, Ecological characteristics, Genetic analysis, Molecular characteristics, Comparison of proteins, Antigen antibody reactions invitro, Nucleic acid base composition, Nucleic acid hybridization, Nucleic acid sequencing are the characteristics used for classification of organisms.

➢ A good classification should bring order to biological diversity and may even clarify the functions of a morphological structure. The best natural classification system may be a phonetic system, which group's organisms based on the mutual similarity of their phenotypic characters.

Sterilization

Introduction

Sterilization means destruction or removal of all life forms from the surface of an object. Microorganisms can be killed, eliminated or inhibited by a number of different physical and chemical means. All the agents that act on microbes are called **anti microbial agents**. Different microbes vary in their susceptibility to anti microbial agents. Choice of an antimicrobial agent depends upon the type of microorganism, its stage of growth, the surrounding in which it is present like air, water, food, sewage, body fluids. Anti microbial agents may affect the functioning of the cell or disrupt its structural organization. Two aspects are to be considered while analyzing the principle of action of anti microbial agents; they are factors concerning the anti microbial agents and factors concerning the microbes to be killed.

Factors concerning antimicrobial agents

a) Heat resistance

Each microorganism has a varying ability to tolerate temperature or heat. Temperature of the reaction medium should be inversely proportional to time i.e. higher the temperature, lesser will be the time required for the killing of microbes. Within the growing range of temperature for microorganisms, a rise of 10°C will increase the effect of anti microbial agents.

Example: Heat resistant endospores of *Clostridium* species may withstand 100°C temperature for 1 hour, but at 119°C they can be killed in 10 minutes.

b) Concentration of chemicals

The concentration also has its own effect in killing the microorganism. If the concentration of anti microbial agent is more, it can result in faster destruction of the microbe.

Example: 0. 1% phenol does not cause any effect on *Escherichia coli*, but 5% phenol can kill *Escherichia coli* in 2 to 3 minutes.

c) Time of action

No anti microbial agent can act instantly. For optimum effect, there should be sufficient time for each anti microbial agent to act on the microbe.

Methods of anti microbial activity

Various methods are used for controlling microbial activity, which eliminates all the microbes. Sterilization is achieved by following methods;

1. Physical methods

2. Chemical methods

3. Ultrasonic methods

4. Radiation methods

Physical Methods

Sterilization by physical methods include killing of microbes by applying moist heat as in steaming or dry heat as in hot air oven or by various methods of filtration to free the medium of microbes.

Physical control with heat

Heat is fast, reliable and relatively inexpensive. It does not introduce chemicals to a substance. When heat is applied above maximum temperature, some biochemical changes will occur in cells organic molecules, which will result in death of the cell. Heat also drives off water, which may be lethal to the cell. The killing rate of heat is related to the function of time and temperature. Each microbial species has a thermal death time (TDT), which is the time necessary for killing it at a given temperature. Each species also has thermal death point (TDP), which is the temperature at which micro organisms will die in a given time. In this method temperature is kept constant and time necessary to kill the cell is determined. TDP is not practiced much, since a particular temperature cannot be lethal at all times and also for all kinds of micro organisms.

Certain factors must be considered for determining the time and temperature for microbial destruction. This includes;

a)   Type of the organism to be killed.

b)   Type of material to be treated

c)   Presence of organic matter.

Direct flame (dry heat)

This is the most rapid method of sterilization. It is also used in the process of incineration. The flame of a Bunsen burner is employed to sterilize bacteriological loops before removing a sample from a culture tube and after preparing a smear. Flaming the tip of the tube also destroys organisms that happen to contact the tip, while burning away lint and dust. Disposable hospital gowns and certain plastic apparatus are materials that may be incinerated

Hot air sterilizer

The hot air sterilizer utilizes radiating dry heat for sterilization. It is also called hot air oven. Hot air oven is used for sterilizing all kinds of laboratory glassware, such as test tubes, pipettes, petri dishes and flasks. The high temperature of the hot airsterilizer can also be used to sterilize other laboratory materials and equipments that are not burned. Hot air oven should not be used to sterilize culture media, as the liquid would boil to dryness.

Figure: Hot air oven.

Moist heat below 100^{0}C

Pasteurization:

Pasteurization of milk is a known example of this method. The temperature employed is either 63^{0}C for 30 minutes (Holder method) or 72^{0}C for 15-20 second (Flash method).

Inspissation:

Heating at 80-85^{0}C for 30 minutes for three successive days. Serum or egg containing media like LJ medium and Loeffler's medium are sterilized by this method.

Moist heat at 100^{0}C

Boiling:

Vegetative bacteria are killed almost immediately at 90-100^{0}C. But spores are not killed.

Steaming:

A single exposure of ninety minutes at 100^{0}C usually kill microorganisms. Arnold steamer is usually used for this process.

Tyndallization:

This method is used for the media containing sugars and gelatin. Exposure of 100^{0}C for 20 minutes for three successive days ensures sterilization.

Moist heat above 100^{0}C

Autoclave

Moist heat in the form of pressurized steam can destroy all forms of life, including bacterial spores. This method is incorporated into a device called the autoclave. It works on the principle of a pressure cooker. Steam when formed in a closed system increases its pressure with increase of temperature. As the water molecules in steam become more energized, their penetration increases substantially. This principle is used to reduce sterilizing time in the autoclave in which the sterilizing agent is moist heat.

An autoclave is a high pressure device used to allow the application of moist heat above the normal atmosphere boiling point of water. Autoclave can sterilize anything that can withstand a temperature of 121°C for 15-20 minutes. The usual working condition in an autoclave is 121^{0}C for 15 -20 minutes at 15 pounds per square inch (psi) pressure.

The autoclave is used to control microbes, in both hospitals and laboratories. It is employed for blankets, bedding, utensils, instruments, intravenous solutions and a broad variety of other objects. It can also be used for sterilizing bacteriological media, and to destroy pathogenic cultures. It cannot be used for sterilizing plastic ware since plastic melts in high temperature. Many chemicals break down during the sterilization process, and oily substances cannot be treated since they do not mix with the water.

Figure: Autoclave

Autoclave control and sterilization indicators

Chemical indicators: Browne's sterilizer control tubes used contain a red solute which turns green when heated at 115^0C for 25 minutes (type 1), for 15 minutes (type 2), or at 160^0C for 60 minutes (type 3).

Adhesive tape: Bowie dick autoclave tapes which changes colour when sufficient temperature is attained in the system.

Spore indicators: A preparation of dried bacterial spores are placed within the load and after autoclaving they are tested for viability. *Bacillus stearothermophilus* are used which are killed at 121^0C in about 12 to 15 minutes.

Filtration

Heat is a valuable physical agent for controlling micro organisms, but heat sensitive solutions cannot be sterilized by using heat. So a heat free process should be used for sterilization. A filter is a mechanical device used for removing micro organisms from a solution. As f luid passes through the filter, organisms are trapped in the pores of the cleaning filter material. The solution that drips into the receiving container is decontaminated or sterilized. Filters are used to sterilize such things as intravenous solutions, bacteriological media, pharmaceutical products and beverages.

Several types of Filters are available for use in the microbiological laboratory. They are:

a. Porcelain or Chamber land filter

b. Berkfeld Filters

c. Mandler Filter

d. Fritted Glass filter

e. Asbestos Filters Jenkins filter

g. Ultra filter

h. Membrane filter

High efficiency particulate air filter (HEPA)

HEPA filters are used to remove microorganism present in air. HEPA filters can remove 99%/o of all particles. The air entering surgical units and specialized wards, such as respiratory disease wards, pharmaceutical-filling rooms etc pass through these filters. Air is recirculated through HEPA filters to ensure its purity.

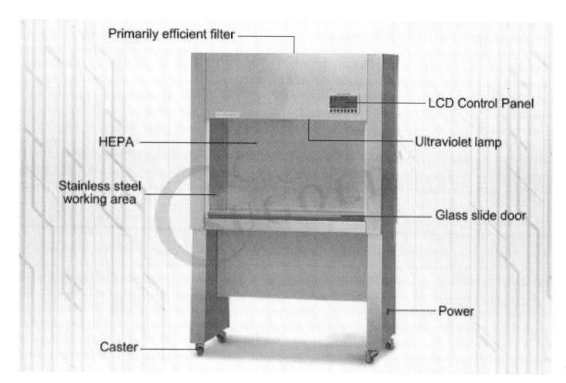

Figure: Laminar air flow hood fitted with HEPA filter

Chemical Methods of Sterilization

Chemical methods are widely used to prevent the spread of disease causing micro organisms, to prevent the growth of microbes that cause spoilage of food and bio deterioration of industrial products. Such chemicals that are used to kill micro organisms and to prevent infection are called antimicrobial agents. There are many different antimicrobial agents that are used to prevent microbial growth. Actively growing micro-organisms are more sensitive than the dormant stages of bacteria. Most of the antimicrobial agents are aimed at blocking the active metabolism and preventing the organism from generating the macromolecular constituents needed for reproduction.

Germicide: It is a chemical gent that kills both pathogenic and non- pathogenic bacteria, but it will not kill the spores.

Bactericide: It is a chemical agent that kills both pathogenic and non- pathogenic bacteria. In practice they are synonymous with germicide.

Antiseptic: Chemical agents that are used to create an aseptic condition. Killing or inhibiting the growth of microorganisms can create aseptic conditions. Aseptic conditions

46

are necessary in hospitals, microbiology laboratories etc. A germicide can also be an antiseptic depending on the strength of the solution, the period of action and the nature of the organism.

Viricide: It is a chemical agent that when applied can inactivate or destroy filterable forms known as viruses.

Fungicides: Chemical agent that can destroy fungi.

Bacteriostatic agent: These are certain chemical agents that can inhibit the growth of bacteria but they do not kill the bacteria.

Properties of a Chemical Agent

a) Microbicidal Activity: A chemical agent must have some anti microbial activity.

b) Stability: The chemical compounds used should not undergo any change on standing for a long time. In any case these changes should not have an adverse effect on the microbicidal properties of the chemical agent.

c) Non-toxicity: The microbicidal chemical should be harmless while handling and non-toxic to human beings and other animals.

d) Solubility: The chemical substance used should be soluble in water or other solvents, which facilitates easy application.

e) Toxicity to microbes under normal temperature: Microbicidal chemicals should be effective under normal ranges of temperature found in the environment.

f) Homogeneity: The microbicidal agent should a homogenous mixture of all chemical irlgredients so that every milliliter of the reagent should have the chemicals in proper proportion.

g) Inability to combine with organic materials: The chemical agents used should have affinity towards proteins and combine. Use of such chemicals will be ineffective if some extraneous proteins are present outside and so the chemical agent becomes non available to kill the microbes.

h) Capacity of penetration: The germicidal chemical should be able to penetrate and percolate into the system, where it is applied and will be more effective.

i) Availability: The chemical used for microbicidal action should be easily available and in sufficient quantity.

j) Deodorisation: The chemical should be able to deodorize the foul smell produced by microbes. The chemical component itself should be odourless or must have a pleasing fragrance.

k) Detergent ability: The chemical agent used should possess detergent properties together with disinfectant ability. This twin action will make the agent more microbicidal.

I) Non-corrosion: An ideal chemical agent should not corrode metallic or other objects and it should not damage any items that they come into contact with.

Chemicals used as antimicrobial agents

Alcohols

Ethyl alcohol (ethanol) and isopropyl alcohol are most frequently used. They are used mainly as skin antiseptics and act by denaturing bacterial proteins. They have no action on spores. To be effective, they must be used at a concentration of 60-70% in water. lsopropyl alcohol is preferred to ethyl alcohol as it is a better fat solvent, more bactericidal and less volatile. It is used for the disinfection of clinical thermometers.

Methyl alcohol is effective against fungal spores and is used for treating cabinets and incubators affected by them.

Aldehydes

Formaldehyde is active against the amino group of the protein molecule. In aqueous solutions, it is markedly bactericidal and sporicidal and also has a lethal effect on viruses. It is used to preserve anatomical specimens and for destroying anthrax spores in hair and wool; 10% formalin containing half percent sodium tetraborate is used to sterilize clean metal instruments.

Formaldehyde gas is used for sterilizing instruments and heat sensitive catheters. It is used for fumigating wards, sick rooms and laboratories. Under properly controlled conditions, clothing, bedding, furniture and books can be satisfactorily disinfected. The gas is irritant and toxic when inhaled.

Glutaraldehyde has an action similar to formaldehyde. It is especially effective against tubercle bacilli, fungi and viruses. It is less toxic and irritant to the eyes and skin than formaldehyde.

Dyes

Two groups of dyes a) the aniline dyes and b) the acridines dyes are used extensively as skin and wound antiseptics. Both have bactericidal activity. The aniline dyes in use are brilliant green, malachite green and crystal violet. They are more active against Gram-positive that Gram-negative organisms. Their lethal effects on bacteria are believed to be due to their reaction with the acid groups in the cell. These dyes are used in the microbiology laboratory as selective agents in culture media.

The acridine dyes are more active against Gram- positive than Gram- negative micro-organisms but are not as selective as the aniline dyes. The more important dyes are proflavine, acriflavine, euflavine and aminacrine.

They show no significant differences in potency. If impregnated in gauze, they are slowly released in moist environment and hence their advantage and use in clinical medicine. They impair the DNA complexes of the organisms and thus kill or destroy the reproductive capacity of the cell.

Halogens

Iodine in aqueous and alcoholic solutions have been used as a skin disinfectant. It is an active bactericidal agent with moderate action against spores. It is active against the tubercle bacillus and a number of viruses. Chlorine and its compounds have been used as disinfectants for many years. Water supplies, Swimming pools, food and dairy industries are some of the areas of their use. Chlorine is used most commonly as hypochlorites. Chlorine and hypochlorites are markedly bactericidal. They have a wide spectrum of action against viruses.

Phenols

The lethal effect of phenols is due to their capacity to cause cell membrane damage, thus releasing cell contents and causing lysis. Low concentrations of phenol precipitate proteins, membrane-bound oxidases and dehydrogene ases which are irreversibly inactivated causing the death of the organism.

Phenol (carbolic acid) is a powerful microbicidal substance. This and other phenolic disinfectants derived from coal tar are widely used as disinfectants for various purposes in hospitals. Lysol and cresol are active against a wide range of organisms. They are not readily inactivated by the presence of organic matter and are thus good general disinfectants. They are markedly toxic to man.

Soap

Soaps are sodium or potassium salts of acids. Consequently, soaps are alkaline (pH greater than 7). Soaps exert their antimicrobial effects in two ways- either by destroying bacteria that are sensitive to high pH or by removing pathogens from surfaces by cleaning the surface.

Detergent

Detergents are synthetic surfactants. There are a variety of structural types of detergents. A detergent may be cationic (positively charged) or anionic (negatively charged). Quaternary ammonium compounds are cationic detergent disinfectants commonly used in hospital practice.

Example : Benzalkonium chloride

Iodine

Iodine is employed as tincture of iodine or as iodophores. Iodine tinctures are used as antiseptics. Iodophores are organic compounds that release iodine in a slow fashion. The iodophores additionally serve as surfactants, thus increasing penetration while simultaneously supplying iodine over long periods.

Example : Betadine

Metallic Salts

The salts of silver, copper and mercury are used as disinfectants. They have the ability for protein coagulations and have the capacity to combine with free sulphydryl groups of cell enzymes, when used at appropriate concentrations. The organic compounds, phenyl mercury nitrate and mercurochrome, are less toxic and are used as mild antiseptics and have a marked bacteriostatic, limited fungicidal and weak bactericidal action. Silver salts in aqueous solution have a limited use. Copper salts are used as fungicides.

These are the various chemical agents that are used as anti microbial agents to prevent the growth and thereby contamination by micro- organisms.

Sterilization by radiation

Ultraviolet light is useful for controlling microorganisms. It has a wavelength of 100 nm to 400 nm. This radiant energy at about 265nm is most destructive to bacteria. When microorganisms are subjected to UV light , the cellular DNA absorbs energy. The adjacent thymine molecules are linked together and form thymidine dimers. Linked thymine molecules are unable to position adenine on mRNA during protein synthesis. Replication of the chromosome is impaired and the damaged organism can no longer produce critical proteins and it gets destroyed. It can be used to destroy air borne or surface contamination in hospital wards, toilets, food service, operation theatres etc. UV light doesn't penetrate liquids or solids and it may damage the human skin cells.

Ionizing radiation

Ionizing radiation is used in various sterilization procedures to kill micro organisms. Viruses as well as other micro organisms are inactivated by exposure to ionizing radiations. Resistance to ionizing radiations is based on the biochemical constituents of a given micro organism. Spores of microorganisms are resistant to radiation. Exposure to 0.3 to 0.4 Mrads (million units of radiation) is necessary to reduce the number of viable spores. Ionizing radiation is used to pasteurize or sterilize some commercial products like plastic petriplates. Most of the sterilization procedures involve exposure to gamma radiation from cobalt 60 or cesium 137.

Microwave radiations, which have longer Wavelength of about 106nm and Infra red radiations, which have a wavelength 103-105 nm, have poor penetrating power. So they do not kill microorganisms directly. Absorption of such long wavelength radiation results in increased temperature and they can indirectly kill microorganisms, because the temperatures are greater than their growth temperatures Since microwaves do not kill microbes directly, food industry has some concern that microbes present in the food products are not adequately killed by microwave oven while cooking.

Ultrasonic Vibrations (non-ionizing radiations)

Ultra sonic vibrations are high frequency sound waves beyond the range of the human ear. When directed against environmental surfaces, they have little value because air particles deflect and disperse the vibration. When the ultrasonic vibrations are propagated in fluids, they cause the formation of microscopic bubbles or cavities and the water appears to boil. So it is also called "cold boiling". The cavities rapidly collapse and send out shock waves. The external pressure quickly disintegrates micro organisms in the fluid. The formation and implosion of the cavities is known as cavitations. This method has got minimal attention as a sterilizing agent because liquid is required and, other methods are much more efficient.

Gaseous sterilization

Heat sterilization is mostly unsuitable for thermolabile solid media and thermolabile equipment, including articles of plastic and delicate rubber items. Sterilization of such material with chemicals in gaseous state finds a greater application. Formaldehyde was previously used as the gaseous agent; nowadays ethylene oxide is the only compound of outstanding importance. Ethylene oxide is the simplest ether and is a colourless gas at room temperature. It is highly inflammable at a concentration of greater than 3°/o in air. So to eliminate the inflammability, it is used in the absence of oxygen. This gas ceases the growth or kills the organism by alkylating the firmly bound sulfydril, imino, carboxy and hydroxy group of proteins and other cellular components. Time of exposure of the gas is inversely proportional to the concentration of ethylene oxide. This gas has a powerful penetrating power, which can affect paper, plastic, fabrics, and rubbers, which are freely permeable to the gas. Presence of organic matter reduces the efficiency of the process. It finds wide application in sterilizing thermo sensitive and thermolabile materials, but the containers carrying these materials are permeable to the gas. It is also a slow process of sterilization. After the sterilization is over, desorption of gas from the material becomes essential. Thus the running cost of the process is high.

Disinfection

It refers to the destruction or removal of all pathogenic microorganisms. Chemical disinfection is commonly used for heat sensitive equipments that are damaged at high temperature.

Ideal disinfectant

> It should be fast acting even in the presence of organic substances, such as those in body fluid; (resistant to inactivation).

> It should be effective against all types of infectious agents without destroying tissues or acting as a poison if ingested; (broadly active).

> It should be easily penetrate material to be disinfected without damaging or discoloring the material (not poisonous or otherwise harmful).

> It should be inexpensive and easy to obtain and use (stable, easily prepared).

> It should not have an unpleasant odor (not unpleasant to work with).

Disinfection of Skin

Washing with soap and water removes most of the transient surface contaminants from skin. A chlorhexidine or iodine detergent should be used if the hands are likely to have become contaminated with pathogens. Unbroken skin should be rinsed with a phenolic or hypochloride disinfectant immediately. If the skin is broken, the wound should be cleaned and irrigated with a mild disinfectant such as chlorhexidine with cetrimide.

Example : Savlon.

Disposal of hospital waste

There are main disposal options of hospital waste are

* Autoclave or decontaminate with chemical disinfectants or boiling for 20 minutes before disposal.

* On site incineration, if possible

* Transportation to distant appropriate facility.

Microbial cultures if disposed off directly may prove fatal to life nearby. So it should be properly sterilized by either autoclaving, dry heat at temperature at $160\text{-}170^{\circ}$ C for 2-4 hours or by incineration.

Short notes

> Sterilization means destruction or removal of all life forms. The principal method of sterilization is by using physical agents such as heat, radiation and filtration. Sterilization by physical methods include killing of microbes by applying moist heat

as in steaming or dry heat as in hot air oven or by various methods of filtration to free the medium of microbes.

- The killing rate of heat is related to the function of time and temperature. Each microbial species has a thermal death time (TDT), which is the time necessary for killing it at a given temperature. Each species also has thermal death point (TDP), which is the temperature at which the micro-organism will die in a given time.

- Hot air oven is used or sterilizing all kinds of laboratory glassware, such as test tubes, pipettes, petri dishes and flasks. The hot air sterilizer is operated at a temperature 160^0 to 180^0C for a period of 1½ hour.

- The autoclave is used to control microbes, in both hospitals and laboratories. It is employed for blankets, bedding, utensils, instruments, intravenous solutions and a broad variety of other objects. It can also be used for sterilizing bacteriological media and to destroy pathogenic and cultures. The autoclave is usually operated at 15 lb steam pressure for a period of 15 minutes, which corresponds to a temperature of 121.6° C. This temperature is sufficient to destroy both vegetative cells and spores in one operation.

- A Filter is mechanical device used for removing micro-organisms from a solution. Filters are used to sterilize such things as intravenous solutions, bacteriological media, pharmaceutical products and beverages.

- UV light defectively reduces microbial population, so it can be used to destroy   air borne or surface contamination in hospital   roads, toilets, food service operation etc.

- Chemical methods are widely used to prevent the spread of disease causing microorganisms, to prevent the growth of microbes that cause spoilage of food, and bio deterioration of industrial products. Such chemicals that are use to kill microorganisms to prevent infection are called antimicrobial agents.

54

- Ethyl alcohol (ethanol) and isopropyl alcohol are the most frequently used bactericidal agents. They are used mainly as skin antiseptics.

- Formaldehyde gas is used for sterilizing instruments and heat sensitive catheters. It is used for fumigating wards, sick rooms and laboratories. Dyes like aniline dyes and the acridine dyes are used extensively as skin and wound antiseptics. Both are having bactericidal activity.

- Iodine is aqueous and alcoholic solutions have been used as a skin disinfectant. Chlorine and its compounds have been used as disinfectants in water supplies swimming pools, food and dairy industries.

Bacteria

Introduction

Bacteria are one of the smallest microorganisms and play a variety of roles, which can be either harmful or beneficial to humans. Useful bacteria play an important role in the preparation of industrially important products. Louis Pasteur is called the "Father of Bacteriology". He was the one who found out that bacteria bring about fermentation. Bacteria are present everywhere, i.e. there is no place free of bacteria. They are present in soil, milk, water, air, temperate regions, tropical regions, in plants, animals, human beings etc. They can withstand different ranges of temperature and are highly adaptable.

Structure of a bacterial cell

Electron microscopic studies have revealed the ultra structure of the bacterial cell. The outer envelope is the cell wall internal to which is the cell membrane. Sometimes external to the cell wall there exists a loose slimy layer or capsule. Some bacteria are flagellate; others have small pili or fimbriae. The bacterial cytoplasm includes ribosomes, mesosomes, fat globules, vacuoles, inclusion bodies and nuclear material.

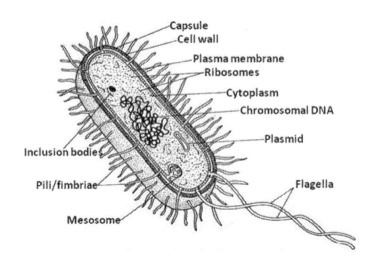

Electron microscopic structure of a typical bacterial cell

Flagella

Flagella are hair like helical appendages that protrude from the cell wall of bacteria. It arises from the basal granule. Numerous species of bacterial rods and spirilla and a limited number of species of cocci are capable of independent movement. To achieve motion, they utilize structures called flagella (sing, flagellum). Flagella are composed of long, rigid strands of a protein called flagellin, Within the strands, the protein exists in ultra thin fibers permanently bent like a coil or helix. This structure permits the flagellum to rotate.

Flagella can vary in number and placement. The flagellum ranges in length from 100μm to 20μm and is there for many times longer than the length of the cell. However, the flagellum is only about 0.2 μm thick and cannot be seen under the light microscope unless coated with dye. In the human body, flagella enable bacteria such as cholera bacilli to move among the tissues and colonize various areas. Some bacteria are known to travel up to 2000 times their own length in an hour.

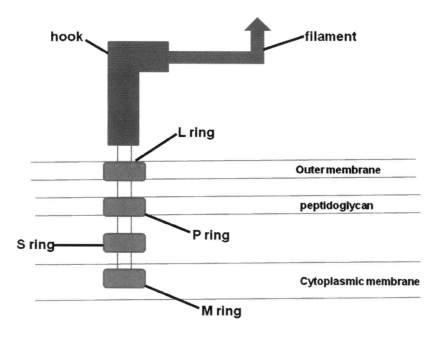

Structure of bacterial flagella

Parts of a flagellum

A flagellum is composed of three basic parts. They are:

a) Filament: The filament is the rigid helical structure that extends from the cell surface. It is composed of the protein flagellin arranged in helical chains so as to form a hollow core.

b) Hook: This is a flexible coupling between the filament and the basal body.

c) Basal body: The basal body consists of a rod and a series of rings that anchor the flagellum to the cell wall and the cytoplasmic membrane. The basal body acts as a molecular motor, enabling the flagellum to rotate and propell the bacterium through the surrounding fluid. Gram positive organisms have 2 basal body rings, one in the peptidoglycan layer and one in the cell membrane. Gram negative organisms have 4 rings; L ring-associated with the tipopolysaccharides, P ring-associated with the peptidoglycan layer, M ring-embedded in the cell membrane, and the S ring- which is directly attached to the cell membrane.

Pili (sing, pilus):

Pili are bacterial appendages that appear as short flagella but have no function in motility. Instead, certain pili aid the transfer of genetic material among bacteria, while other pili anchor bacteria to surfaces such as living tissue. By doing so, pili enhance an organisms ability to cause disease. Pili are primarily found on Gram-negative bacteria such as *Neisseria gonorrhoeae*, the cause of gonorrhea. Pili are composed of a protein called pilin, so the body's immune system responds to their presence by producing anti pilli antibodies. It should be noted that some microbiologists use the word fimbriae (sing. fimbria) to refer to bacterial structures of attachment and reserve the word pili for structures that function in genetic transfers. Sex pili help in the conjugation process, during which it can transfer the genetic material. Sex pili is also called F-pili or fertility factor. Some pili may play a major role in human infection in which they get attached to the cell linings and are thus prevented from being washed away by the flow of mucous or body fluids and permits the infection to be established.

Capsule

Many species of bacteria secrete a layer of polysaccharides and small proteins that adheres to the bacterial surface. Commonly known as a capsule, this layer is a very sticky, gelatinous structure formed by various species of bacilli and cocci, but not by spiral bacteria. The capsule serves as a buffer between the cell and its external environment. Because of its high water content, the capsule protects the cell against dehydration while preventing nutrients from flowing away.

In the body, it also contributes to the establishment of diseases because white blood cells that normally engulf and destroy bacteria by phagocytosis cannot perform the function on encapsulated bacteria. For example, *Streptococcus pneumoniae* a principal cause of bacterial pneumonia is very pathogenic in its encapsulated form but harmless when the capsule has been experimentally removed. Most of the bacterial capsules is composed of polysaccharide. It can be a heteropolysaccharide E.g. *Klebsiella pneumoniae* or a homopolysaccharide. E.g. *Streptococcus* mutans. In some cases the capsule is made up of polypeptides. E.g. *Bacillus anthracis*. When the capsule has a looser consistency and is less tightly bound to the cell. It is commonly referred to as a slime layer, or glycocalyx. This structure usually contains a mass of tangled fibers of a polysaccharide catled dextran. The capsule can be observed under the light microscope by a special staining technique called negative staining by Indian ink. Under the light microscope the capsule appears as an amorphous gelatinous area surrounding the cell.

Functions of capsule

a) Provide protection against temporary drying by binding to water molecules.

b) Block attachment of Bacteriophages

c) Inhibit the engulfment of pathogenic bacteria by white blood cells, which contributes to virulence.

d) Promote attachment of bacteria to surfaces.

e) Promote the stability of the bacterial suspension by preventing the cells from aggregating and settling down, due to the electric charge of the surface.

Cell wall

All bacteria have a cell wall, which protects the cell and determines its shape. The most important chemical constituent of the bacterial cell wall is the peptidoglycan. This is a very large molecule composed of alternating units of two amino group containing carbohydrates N-acetyl muramic acid and N-acetyl glucosamine, joined by cross bridges of amino acids. Peptidoglycan can occur in multiple layers connected by side chains of four amino acids. With the notable exception of mycolplasma, all bacteria have a cell wall. This structure protects the cell and to a large extent, determines its shape.

The cell walls of Gram-positive and Gram-negative bacteria differ considerably. In Gram-positive bacteria, the peptidoglycan layer is about 25 nm wide and contains an additional polysaccharide called techoic acid. About 60 to 90 percent of the cell wall is peptidoglycan, and the material is so abundant that Gram-positive bacteria are able to retain the crystal violet- iodine complex during Gram staining.

In contrast, Gram-negative bacteria have a peptidoglycan layer only 3nm wide with no techoic acid. The cell wall in these bacteria contains various polysaccharides, proteins and lipids and is much more complex than the cell wall of Gram-positive bacteria. Also, an outer membrane barely separated from the cell wall by a so-called periplasmic space containing a gel-like material called periplasm surrounds the cell wall. On the inner side of the cell wall the periplasmic space is wider. Bacterial toxins and enzymes apparently remain in this space and destroy antibacterial substances before they can affect the cell membrane. Other proteins facilitate passage through the cell membrane. The multiple layers of the Gram-negative cell also afford protection by restricting the passage of chemicals such as antibiotics, salts and dyes to the cell. The crystal violet-iodine complex in Gram staining is lost partly because of the thinness of the cell wall in Gram-negative bacteria. The cell wall holds the cell together. It also prevents the cell from bursting.

Outer membrane is a bilayered membrane consisting of phospholipid, protein, and lipopolysaccharide. The toxic property of the cell wall is mediated by the lipopolysaccharide.

Lipopolysaccharide consists of three parts i.e. lipid A, core polysaccharide and polysaccharide (o) side chanis (o-antigens). Outer membrane also allows some small molecules like peptides and amino acids to pass through it through channels called porins.

Significance of lipopolysaccharide

a) Avoids host defenses, due to the presence of the o-side chain

b) Stabilizes the cell membrane structure

c) Secretes endotoxins that lead to symptoms of some diseases

d) It acts as a protective barrier

e) It prevents the entry of antibiotics or bile salts into the bacterial cell.

Protoplast

A protoplast is a bacterial cell without the cell wall and consists of only the cytoplasmic membrane and cell material bounded by it. Protoplasts can be prepared from Gram-positive bacteria by treating the cells with lysozyme, which will dissolve the cell wall. It can also be prepared by culturing the bacteria in presence of an antibiotic like penicillin, which prevents the formation of the cell wall.

Spheroplast:

These are round and osmotically fragile forms of Gram-negative bacteria. It can be prepared by the same methods that are used for the Gram-positive bacteria.

Cell membrane

The cell membrane (also called the plasma membrane) is the boundary layer of the bacterial cell. Some microbiologists combine the cell membrane, cell wall and capsule (if present) together as a group and term them the "cell envelope".

Approximately 60 percent of the cell membrane is composed of protein and about 40 percent of lipid, mainly phospholipid. The phospholipid molecules are arranged in two parallel layers (a phospholipid bilayer) one at the outside, the other at the inside of the membrane. In contrast, the proteins are arranged as globules floating like icebergs at or near the inner and outer surfaces of the membrane and some globules extend from one surface of the membrane to the other. This model of the membrane, called the fluid mosaic model, accounts for the membrane's appearance under the electron microscope and helps to explain how it allows passage of certain substances.

Functions of cell membrane

a) Transport nutrients into the cell and waste materials outside the cell.

b) Anchor DNA during replication and it is the site for enzyme synthesis.

c) Links cell with the environment.

d) Selectively permeable and it acts as a barrier.

e) Retains the cytoplasm particularly in cells without cell walls.

Cytoplasm

Cytoplasm lies inside the cell membrane, a gelatinous mass of proteins, carbohydrates, lipids, nucleic acids, salts and inorganic ions all dissolved in water. Cytoplasm is the foundation substance of a cell and the center of its growth and biochemistry. It is thick, semitransparent and elastic. Many cellular structures are found in the cytoplasm and are called cytoplasmic organelles. Bacteria do not contain all the cytoplasmic organelles present in eukaryotes. Main cellular organelles present are the ribosomes, and the nuclear material is made up of DNA. It does not contain a well-defined nuclear membrane enveloping the nuclear material. Mesosomes are certain invaginations of the plasma membrane, which project into the cytoplasm.

Ribosomes are cytoplasmic bodies of RNA and are associated with the synthesis of protein. Other bodies found in various bacteria include globules of starch; these globules store nutrients for later use during periods of starvation. Metachromatic granules / Volutin granules, are phosphate depots that stain deeply with dyes like methylene blue. They are present in diphtheria a bacillus, which helps in the identification procedures. A recently discovered body, the magnetosome, helps certain bacteria orient themselves to the environment. Crystals of an iron-containing compound called magnetite fill the magnetosome and align themselves with the local magnetic field. Scientists believe that the magnetite directs bacteria toward their habitat. It also contains Poly Hydroxy Butyrate crystals (PHB) as a reservoir of carbon and energy source, glycogen granules and sulphur globules.

The cytoplasm is also houses the bacterial chromosome, which contains the hereditary information of the cell. It is suspended in the cytoplasm without a covering or membrane and is not associated with proteins. The term nucleoid is applied to the chromosome region. Plasmids are certain small molecules of DNA, which exists as closed circular loops. They contain few genes that are responsible for antibiotic resistance. So they are called R-factors

(Resistance factors). Plasmids may be transferred between cells during recombination processes and are known to multiply during cell division or reproduction.

Bacterial Spores

These are highly resistant structures and are metabolically dormant form which can undergo germination and outgrowth to form a vegetative cell under appropriate conditions. Bacterial spores remain alive in boiling water i.e. 100^0 Celsius for 2 hours. It can withstand radiation; drying etc. The spores present within bacteria are called endospores. They are retractile and thick walled bodies that are produced by bacteria inside its body.

Examples for spore forming Bacteria:

Bacillus anthracis, Clostridium tetani, Sporosarcina.

Bacterial genetic material

Bacterial genetic material exists in two forms as chromosome or as independent extranuclear material i.e. plasmid

Chromosome

It is usually single circular molecule of double stranded DNA. Length of the chromosome is often more than the length of the cell. So it is coiled in such a way as to fit into the cell. Hence it is regarded to be in super coiled state.

Plasmid

Plasmids are extra chromosomal DNA, which is much smaller in size than the chromosome. These include non-essential genes that would be advantageous under certain conditions e.g. the genes for added virulence and antibiotic resistance. Molecular biologists use plasmids as vectors for genetic engineering.

Gene transfer in bacteria

New genotypes arise when genetic material transferred from one bacterium to another. The transferred DNA can recombine with genome of the recipient cell. If the transferred DNA is on plasmid, it can undergo replication without recombination. DNA can be transferred from one cell to another by four processes

a) Transformation b) Transduction c) Conjugation d) Transposition

Transformation

It is simply the process, where bacteria manage to uptake or bring in a piece of external DNA. Usually this process is used in the laboratory to introduce a small piece of plasmid DNA into a bacterial cell. The first demonstration of bacterial transformation was done by Frederick Griffith.

Transduction

It is the transfer of a portion of bacterial genetic material from one bacterium (donor) to another recipient through viruses or called as bacteriophage. During the process of bacteriophage infection, other DNA in the cell (genomic or plasmid) is occasionally erroneously packaged into the virus head resulting in a transducing particle which can attach to and transfer the DNA into the recipient cell. This transduced genetic material could confer some additional properties like production of toxin or resistance to antibiotics.

There are two very different kinds of transduction a) Generalized transduction b) Specialized transduction.

Generalized transduction

If all fragments of bacterial DNA (from any region of the bacterial chromosome) have a chance to enter a transducing phage, the process is called generalized transduction.

Specialized transduction

In specialized transduction, certain temperate phage strains can transfer only a few restricted genes of the bacterial chromosome. More specifically the phages transducers only those bacterial genes adjacent to the prophage in the bacterial chromosome.

Conjugation

Conjugation is a process in which there is a unidirectional transfer of genetic information through direct cellular contact between a donor and a recipient bacterial cell. The donor state is conferred by the presence of a plasmid called an F factor. The pilus will attach to the other bacteria and form the conjugation bridge through which genetic exchange takes place.

Transposition

Movement of genetic information between DNA molecules of the same cell is called as transposition. Transposable elements are DNA sequences can jump and transpose from one site of DNA molecule to another in the cell. They are also referred to as jumping genes.

Bacterial reproduction and growth

Bacteria reproduce by an asexual process called binary fission. In this sequence of events, the chromosome duplicates, the cell elongates, and the plasma membrane pinches inwards at the center of the cell. When the nuclear material has been evenly distributed, the cell wall thickens and grows inward to separate the dividing cell. No mitotic structures (e.g., spindle, asters) are present as in eukaryotic cells. Reproduction by binary fission lends a certain immorality to the bacteria because there is never a moment at which the first bacterium has died. Bacteria mature, undergo binary fission, and are young again. The interval of time until the completion of the next division is known as the generation time. In some bacteria, the generation time is very short; for others it is quite long. For example, for *Staphylococcus aureus*, the generation time is about 30 minutes; for Mycobacterium tuberculosis, the agent of tuberculosis, it is approximately 18 hours; for Escherichia coli generation time is 20 minutes and for, *Treponema pallidum*, the syphilis spirochete it is as long 33 hours. The generation time is the determining factor in the amount of time that passes before disease symptoms appear in an infected individual.

Classification of bacteria

Bacteria are classified into different groups based on certain characteristics. They can be classified:

a)   **Based on the shape and arrangement**

b)   **Based on the nutritional characteristics**

c)   **Based on staining characteristics.**

d)   **Based on the presence of flagella**

a)   **Based on shape and arrangement**

Bacteria are classified into different groups based on their cell shape. They are bacilli, cocci, vibrio, spirochetes, spirilla, actinomycetes and mycolplasma. The type of cellular arrangement of bacteria is determined by the plane through which binary fission takes place and also by the tendency of the daughter cells to remain attached even after division.

Bacilli: The rod shaped bacteria are known as a bacillus (pl., bacilli). In various species of bacteria, they vary in their length from 0.5µm to 20µm. Certain rods such as those of typhoid fever are slender; others such as the agents of anthrax are rectangular with squared ends; still others such as diphtheria bacilli are club shaped. Most rods occur singly, but some form long chains called streptobacilli.

The bacilli are arranged in different forms.
a) They are arranged singly e.g. *Clostridium tetani, Corynebacterium diphtheriae.*
b) Bacilli arranged in pairs are called diplobacilli. E.g. *Escherichia coli*
c) Bacilli arranged in chains are called streptobacilli. E.g. *Anthrax bacilli*

Cocci: Spherical shaped bacteria are called cocci. They are the smallest among bacteria. This term derived from the Greek word 'kokos' means "berry". They are usually round, other forms like oval shaped bacteria are also present. Cocci are also arranged in different forms, which include:

a) Cocci in chains are called Streptococci. E.g. Streptococcus pyogenes. Certain streptococci are involved in throat and tooth decay, but many are harmless enough to be used for producing dairy products such as yogurt.

b) Cocci that occur in clusters are called Staphylococci. Cocci divide randomly and form an irregular grapelike cluster of cells called staphylococci, from "staphyle", the Greek word for "grape". Staphylococcus is an important pathogenic organism, which can cause food poisoning, toxic shock syndrome (TSS) and numerous skin infections. E.g. Staphylococcus aureus, Staphylococcus epidermidis.

Another variation of cocci is called a sarcina. The sarcina is a cube like packet of eight cocci. (Sarcina in Latin means bundle). E.g. Micrococcus luteus is a sarcina, which is a common inhabitant of the skin.

Vibrios: are comma shaped bacilli. One major member among this group is called Vibrio cholerae, commonly called cholera bacilli, and it causes cholera. The name of vibrio is derived from the characteristic vibratory motility of the bacteria.

Spirochetes: are flexible spiral forms of bacteria. They have flexible cell wall and no flagella. Movement in this organism occurs by contractions of the long filaments (endo flagella) that run along the length of the cell wall.

E.g. *Treponema pallidum*

Spirilla: Rigid spiral shaped bacteria are called spirilla. They have a rigid cell wall and hair like projections called flagella, which help in their movement. E.g. Spirillum minus.

Actinomycetes: They are branching filamentous bacteria. They have a particular shape due to the presence of a rigid cell wall.

Mycoplasma: These groups of bacteria are cell wall deficient bacteria, so they do not possess a stable morphology. They occur as round or oval bodies and as interlacing filaments.

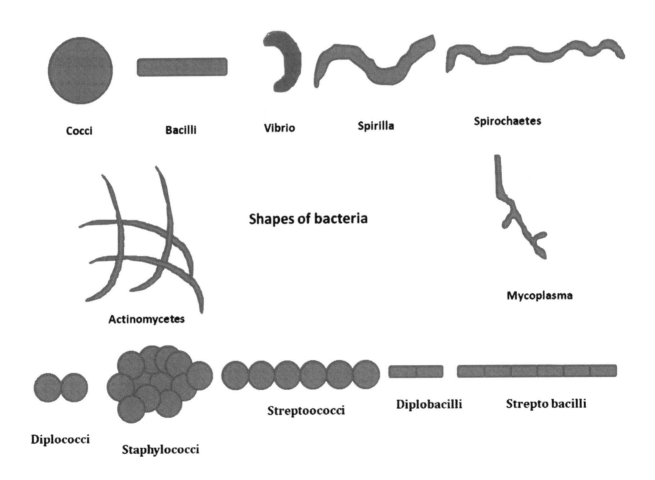

Figure: Classification of bacteria based on shape and arrangement

b) Based on the nutritional characteristics

Bacteria require nutrients for their growth and development. These nutrients include macronutrients and micronutrients. The macronutrients / major elements are to be produced in large amounts. This includes carbon, nitrogen, hydrogen, oxygen, sulphur, phosphorous, potassium, calcium, magnesium and iron. The micronutrients include zinc, cobalt, molybdenum, nickel, copper and manganese. These elements form part of enzymes and cofactors. Mainly bacteria need a source of carbon, energy and electrons to carry out their metabolic activities and bacteria have been classified into six following categories.

i) **autotrophs** ii) **heterotrophs** iii) **phototrophs** iv) **chemotrophs** v) **organotrophs** vi) **lithotrophs**

i) Autotrophs: Microbes that obtain their carbon from carbon dioxide are termed as autotrophs.

ii) Heterotrophs: Microbes that obtain their carbon from pre-made organic compounds in the environment are termed as heterotrophs.

iii) Phototrophs: Microbes need energy for carrying out cellular reactions comes either from the conversion of light energy or by the oxidation of chemicals. Those organisms which utilize light as a source of energy are called as phototrophs.

iv) Chemotrophs: They obtain energy by the oxidation of either inorganic or organic compounds.

v) Organotrophs: For metabolic reactions, a source of electrons is also necessary and microbes that obtain their electrons from organic compounds are termed organotrophs.

vi) Lithotrophs: These are also called as rock eaters. These obtain electrons from inorganic compounds to carry out metabolic reactions in cell, are called lithotrophs.

By combining the above sets of terms bacteria are again classified into 4 categories according to their nutritional requirements

a) **Photoautotrophs** b) **Photoheterotrophs** c) **Chemoautotrophs** d) **Chemoheterotrophs**

Photoautotrophs:

Photoautotrophs use light as a source of energy and carbon dioxide as their chief source of carbon. They include photosynthetic bacteria (green and purple bacteria and Cyanobacteria), Algae, and green plants, the hydrogen atoms of water are used to reduce carbondioxide, and oxygen gas is given off. Because this photosynthetic process produces O_2, it is sometimes

68

called oxygenic. The chlorophylls used by these photosynthetic bacteria are called bacteriochlorophylls, and they absorb light at longer wavelengths than that absorbed by chlorophyll a. Bacteriochlorophylls of green sulfur bacteria are found in vesicles called chlorosomes (or Chlorobium vesicles) underlying and attached to the plasma membrane. In the purple sulfur bacteria, the bacteriochlorophylls are located in invaginations of the plasma membrane (intracytoplasmic membranes). Several characteristics distinguish eukaryotic photosynthesis from prokaryotic photosynthesis.

Photoheterotrophs

Photoheterotrophs use light as a source of energy but cannot convert carbon dioxide to sugar; rather, they use organic compounds, such as alcohols, fatty acids, carbohydrates and other organic compounds, as sources of carbon. They are anoxygenic. The green nonsulfur bacteria such as Chloflexus and purple nonsulfur bacteria, such as Rhodopseudomas are photoheterotrophs. Heterotrophs are further classified according to their source of organic molecules. Saprophytes live on dead organic matter and parasites derive organic matter from a living host. Most bacteria, and all fungi, protozoa and animals are chemoheterotrophs. Prototrophs are microorganisms that require same nutrients as most of the naturally occurring members of its species. It get mutated, so cannot synthesize a molecule that can be converted to a nutrient.

Chemoautotrophs

Chemoautotrophs use the electrons from reduced inorganic compounds as a source of energy and use CO_2 as their principal source of carbon. Inorganic sources of energy for these organisms include hydrogen sulfide (H_2S) for *Beggiatoa*; elemental sulfur (S) for *Thiobacillus thioxidans*; ammonia (NH_3) for *Nitrosomonas*; nitrite ions (NO_2-) for *Nitrobacter*; hydrogen gas (H_2) for *Hydrogenomonas*; ferrous ion (F^{2+}) for *Thiobacillus ferroxidans*; and carbon monoxide (CO) for *Pseudomonas carboxydohydrogena*.

Chemoheterotrophs

Chemoheterotrophs depend upon organic compounds as a source of energy, source of carbon and also source of electron. Most bacteria and some archaea are belong to this category.

Table: Types of bacteria according to their nutritional requirements

Type	Carbon source	Energy source	Electron source	Examples

Photoautotrophs	CO_2	Sun light	Inorganic compound	Cyanobacteria
Photoheterotrophs	Organic compound	Sun light	Organic compound	Purple and green bacteria
Chemoautotrophs	CO_2	Chemical compound	Inorganic compound	Bacteria and many archaea
Chemoheterotrophs	Organic compound	Organic compound	Organic compound	Most bacteria, some archaea

c)   Based on staining characteristics

Based on the Gram staining technique, bacteria are classified into two different groups. They are: Gram negative bacteria and Gram positive bacteria. Most bacteria come under any of the two staining types. Gram- negative bacteria will appear bright red or magenta colored because it takes up the counter stain saffranine. Gram-positive bacteria will appear violet colored because the cells take up the primary stain, which is crystal violet.

E.g. Gram Positive Bacteria: *Anthrax bacilli, Staphylococcus aureus*.

E.g. Gram Negative Bacteria: *Escherichia coli*.

d)   Based on the presence of flagella

The arrangement of flagella is characteristic of a species and is used in classifying the species in taxonomic schemes. They are classified as a) monotrichous, b) lophotrichous, c) amphitrichous, d) peritrichous e) atrichous

a) Monotrichous bacterium (a montrichaete) possesses a single flagellum at any one pole, E.g. *Pseudomonas aeruginosa*.

b) Lophotrichous bacterium (a lophotrichaete) has a group of two or more flagella at one pole of the cell. E.g. *Pseudomonas fluorescence*.

c) An amphitrichous bacterium (an amphitrichate) has groups of flagella at both ends, E.g. *Aquaspirillum serpenes*.

d) Peritrichous bacterium (a peritrichaete) is covered with flagella all over the body. E.g. *Salmonella typhi*

e) Atrichous bacterium: Bacteria that do not posses flagella.

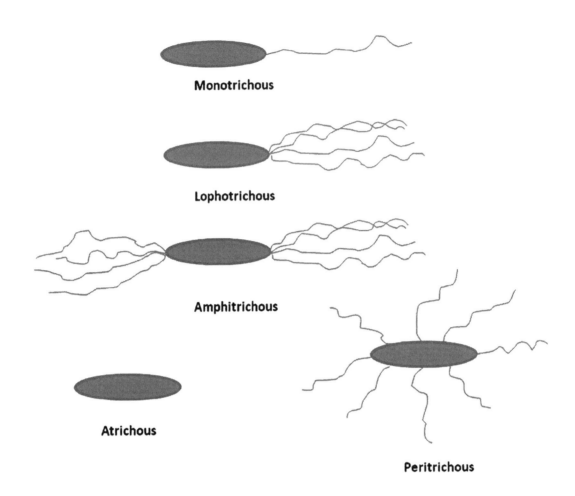

Monotrichous

Lophotrichous

Amphitrichous

Atrichous

Peritrichous

Classification of bacteria on the presence of flagella

Bacterial reproduction and growth

Bacteria reproduce by an asexual process called binary fission. In this sequence of events, the chromosome duplicates, the cell elongates, and the plasma membrane pinches inwards at the center of the cell. When the nuclear material has been evenly distributed, the cell wall thickens and grows inward to separate the dividing cell. No mitotic structures (e.g., spindle, asters) are present as in eukaryotic cells. Reproduction by binary fission lends a certain immorality to the bacteria because there is never a moment at which the first bacterium has died. Bacteria mature, undergo binary fission, and are young again. The interval of time until the completion of the next division is known as the generation time. In some bacteria, the generation time is very short; for others it is quite long. For example, for *Staphylococcus aureus*, the generation time is about 30 minutes; for *Mycobacterium tuberculosis*, the agent of tuberculosis, it is approximately 18 hours; for *Escherichia* coli generation time is 20 minutes and for, *Treponema pallidum*, the syphilis spirochete it is as long 33 hours. The generation time is the determining factor in the amount of time that passes before disease symptoms appear in an infected individual.

Normal flora in human body

Human body has more bacterial cells than human cells. Human body is made up of about 10^{13} number of cells, but approximately 10^{14} number of bacteria are present in human body. This group of bacteria are called as normal flora which is composed of mostly anaerobic bacteria.

Distribution of normal flora

Skin flora

The bulk of the human skin surface is predominantly inhabited by *Staphylococcus epidermidis* and *Propionibacterium.* Areas such as the axilla (armpit) and the perineum (groin) provide typically moister region for bacterial growth. These environments often harbor the largest diversity amongst the skin flora. Organisms include Staphylococcus aureus, Corynebacterium species and some species of Gram-negative bacteria.

Oral cavity and nasopharyngeal flora

In the oral cavity region, species of Streptococci are found, where as in nasopharyngeal regions many pathogens are found. These pathogens include *Streptococcus pneumoniae*, *Neisseria meningitides* and *Haemophilus influenza.*

Intestinal Flora

The large intestine may contain 10^9 to 10^{11} bacteria per gram of the material. Most of these are anaerobes such as *Bacteroids*, *Bifidobacterium*, anaerobic *Streptococci* and *Clostridium.* These organisms inhibit the growth of other pathogens.

Urogenital Flora

The urogenital tract is normally sterile with the exception of the vagina and the distal 1 cm of the urethra. Lactobacillus species predominate in the vagina. These organisms lower the pH to around 4-5, which is optimal for the lactobacilli but inhibitory for the growth of many other bacteria. The urethra may contain predominantly skin flora including *Staphylococci, Streptococci* and *Diptheroids*.

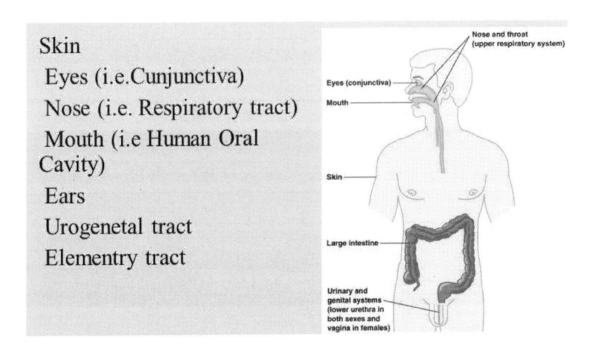

Figure: Normal flora of human body

Advantages of normal flora

Normal flora synthesizes vitamins. For example, enteric bacteria secrete Vitamin K and Vitamin B12, and lactic acid bacteria produce certain B-vitamins. The normal flora prevent colonization by pathogens by competing for attachment sites or for essential nutrients. This is thought to be their most important beneficial effect, which has been demonstrated in the oral cavity, the intestine, the skin and the vaginal epithelium.

Disadvantages of normal flora

Normal flora harms us by causing diseases especially when our immune system is compromised. Although these organisms are non-pathogenic in their usual anatomic location, they can be pathogenic in other parts of the body.

Bacterial growth

Bacteria grow by binary fission; one cell grows and divides into two identical daughter cells. Bacteria require certain nutrients for its growth. Apart from nutrients they also require optimal pH, temperature and other growth conditions.

Nutrients

Bacteria need a source of carbon, nitrogen, phosphorus, sulphur and other trace materials. Besides that a wide range of compounds are needed. Those are sugars and carbohydrates, amino acids, sterols, alcohols, hydrocarbons, methane, inorganic salts and carbon dioxide. Water is needed for growth and reproduction as 80% of the mass of typical bacteria is water. All bacteria need low concentrations of inorganic ions in order to function, such as iron for cytochromes and certain enzymes, magnesium for cell wall stability, manganese and nickel in metabolic enzymes.

Growth curve

It is the curve plotted by taking count of bacteria at different intervals in relation to time. A growth curve has four phases such as lag phase, exponential phase/log phase, stationary phase and death phase.

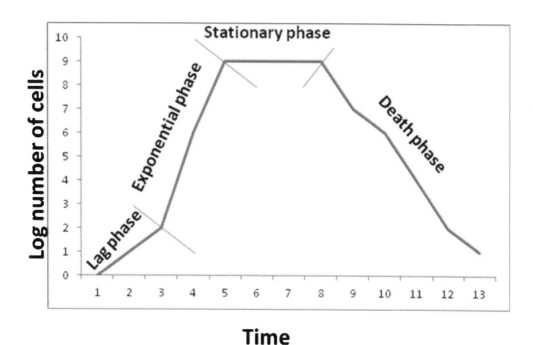

Bacterial growth curve showing four phases

74

Lag phase

It is the initial time interval just after inoculation of bacteria to liquid medium. Bacteria need time to regenerate essential nutrients before growth can resume, requires new enzyme synthesis and time for pathways to function.

Exponential phase/ Log phase

In this stage cells are in optimum growth state, divide repeatedly by binary fission at maximal rate. This phase is also called as Log phase.

Stationary phase

This phase results from exhaustion of some critical nutrient, or to accumulation of waste products that slow down growth (e.g. acid buildup from fermentation).

Death phase

This phase results from continuous accumulation of wastes, exposure to oxygen, loss of cells ability to detoxify toxins.

Continuous culture

The liquid culture that routinely employ in a laboratory are called batch cultures in which nutrients are not renewed, exponential growth is limited to a few generations. In the other hand, bacteria cultures can be maintained in a state of exponential growth over long periods of time using a system of continuous culture. Chemostat is a device which is used to maintain a bacterial population at a constant density, a situation that is in many ways more similar to bacterial growth in natural environments.

Short notes

- Microbiology is the branch of biology that deals with the study of small organisms that can be seen only under the microscope. Such organisms are called microorganisms, and are believed to be the primitive forms of life. They include many organisms like bacteria, virus, fungi etc.

- Bacteria are one of the smallest microorganisms and play variety of roles, which are either harmful or beneficial to humans, Louis Pasteur is called the "Father of Bacteriology".

- Bacteria are classified into different groups based on different characteristics. They are based on shape and arrangement, nutritional characteristics, presence of flagella, and staining characteristics. Bacteria are classified into different groups based on the is shape. They are cocci, bacilli, vibrio, spirochetes, spirilla, actinomycetes and mycoplasma.

- Based on the gram staining technique, bacteria are classified into two different groups. They are: Gram Negative Bacteria and Gram Positive Bacteria.

- Electron microscopic studies have revealed the ultra structure of the bacterial cell. The outer envelope is the cell wall internal to which is the cell membrane. Sometimes external to the ceil wall there will be a loose slimy layer or capsule. Some bacteria are flagellate; others have small pili or fimbriae. The bacterial cytoplasm includes ribosomes, mesosomes, fat globules, vacuoles, inclusion bodies and nuclear material.

- Flagella are hair like helical appendages that protrude from the cell wall of bacteria.

- Pili (sing, pilus) are bacterial appendages that appear as short flagella but have no function in motility. Capsule, is a very sticky, gelatinous structure formed by various species of bacilli and cocci.

- Cell wall protects the cell and determines its shape. The most important chemical constituent of the bacterial cell wall is the peptidoglycan.

- The cell membrane (also called the plasma membrane) is the boundary layer of the bacterial cell.

Viruses

Viruses do not fall strictly into the category of unicellular microorganisms, as they do not possess a cellular organization. They contain only one type of nucleic acid, either DNA or RNA but never both. They are obligate intracellular parasites. They lack the enzymes necessary for protein and nucleic acid synthesis and are dependent for replication on the synthetic machinery of host cells. These are the smallest living units of life.

Morphology

Viruses are much smaller than bacteria. It was their small size and filterability (ability to pass through filters that can hold back bacteria) that led to their recognition as a separate class of infectious agents. Viruses are varying widely in size. The largest virus poxvirus measuring about 300 nm are large as the smallest bacteria i.e. mycoplasma. The smallest virus parvovirus measuring about 20 nm are nearly as small as the largest protein molecule such as hemocyanin.

Structure and shape

The virus consists essentially of a nucleic acid core surrounded by a protein coat, known as the capsid. The capsid with the enclosed nucleic acid is known as the nucleocapsid. The function of the capsid is to protect the nucleic acid from inactivation by nucleases and other deleterious agents in the environment. The capsid is composed of a large number of capsomers. The chemical units of the capsid are polypeptide molecules, which are arranged systematically to form an impenetrable shell around the nucleic acid core. One of the major functions of the capsid is to introduce the viral genome into host cells by adsorbing readily to cell surfaces.

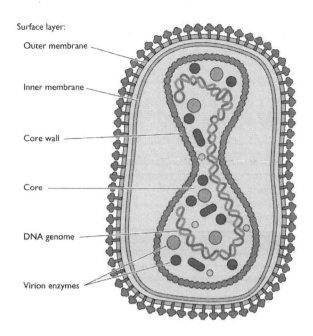

Surface layer:

Outer membrane

Inner membrane

Core wall

Core

DNA genome

Virion enzymes

Structure of a virus

Viral symmetry

Two kinds of symmetry are met within the capsid; they are icosahedral and helical symmetry. Icosahedrons are polygon with 12 vertices or corners and 20 facets or sides. Each facet is in the shape of an equilateral triangle. Two types of capsomers constitute the icosahedral capsid. They are the pentagonal capsomers at the vertices (pentons) and the hexagonal capsomers making up the facets (hexons). There are always 12 pentons but the number of hexons varies with the virus group. In the nucleocapsid with helical symmetry, the capsomers and nucleic acid are wound together to form a helical or spiral tube. Not all viruses show the typical icosahedral or helical symmetry. Some like the poxviruses exhibit a complex symmetry.

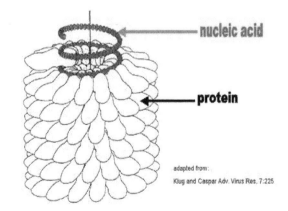

nucleic acid

protein

adapted from :
Klug and Caspar Adv. Virus Res, 7:225

Helical structure of tobacco mosaic virus

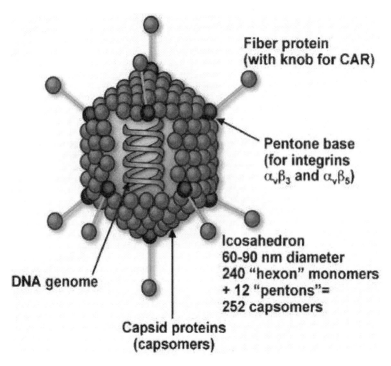

Icosahedral structure of virus

The overall shape of the virus particle varies in different group of viruses. Most animal viruses are roughly spherical. Some are irregular and pleomorphic. The rabies virus is bullet shaped and poxviruses are brick shaped. The tobacco mosaic virus (TMV) is rod shaped. Bacterial viruses have a complex morphology. They may be enveloped or non-enveloped. The envelope or outer covering of viruses is derived from the host cell membrane when the progeny virus is released by budding. The envelope is lipoprotein in nature. The lipid is largely of host cell origin while the protein is virus coded. Protein subunits may be seen as projecting spikes on the surface of the envelope. These structures are called peplomers. A virus may have more than one type of peplomers. Envelopes confer chemical, antigenic and biological properties on viruses.

Chemical properties of viruses

Viruses contain only one type of nucleic acids, either single or double stranded DNA or RNA. In this respect, viruses are unique, for nowhere else in nature does RNA solely carry genetic information. Viruses also contain protein, which makes up the capsid. Enveloped viruses contain lipids derived from the host cell membrane. Some viruses also contain small amounts of carbohydrate. Most viruses do not posses any enzymes for the synthesis of viral components or for energy production.

Resistance

With few exceptions, viruses are very heat labile. There are individual variations but in general they are inactivated within seconds at 56° Celsius, in some minutes at 37° Celsius. They are stable at low temperatures. For long-term storage, they are kept frozen at -70° Celsius. A better method for prolonged storage is lyophilisation or freeze drying. Viruses vary greatly in their resistance to acidity. All viruses are disrupted under alkaline conditions. Sunlight, UV rays and ionizing radiations inactivate viruses. They are in general, more resistant than bacteria to chemical disinfectants, probably because they lack enzymes. Phenolic disinfectants are only weakly virucidal. The most active antiviral disinfectants are oxidizing agents such as hedrogen peroxide, potassium permanganate and hypochlorites. Organic iodine compounds are actively virucidal. Formaldehyde and beta propiolactone actively virucidal and are commonly employed for the preparation of killed viral vaccines. The action of lipid solvents such as ether, chloroform and bile salts is selective, the enveloped viruses being sensitive and naked viruses resistant to them.

Viral multiplication

The genetic information necessary for viral replication is contained in the viral nucleic acid. The virus depends on the synthetic machinery of the host cell for replication. There are general similarities in the pattern of multiplication of bacterial and animal viruses, there are also important differences. The viral multiplication cycle can be divided into six sequential phases, though the phases may sometimes be overlapping. This replicative cycle in bacteriophages is called the lytic cycle.

Different steps in the lytic cycle are

1. Adsorption or attachment
2. Penetration
3. Uncoating
4. Biosynthesis
5. Maturation
6. Release of progeny

Attachment

Virions may come into contact with cells by random collision but adsorption takes place only if there is an affinity between the two. The cell surface should contain specific receptor sites to which the virus can gain attachments. Differences in susceptibility to virus infection are to a large extend based on the presence or absence of receptors on cells.

Penetration

Bacteria possess rigid cell walls. Bacterial viruses cannot therefore penetrate into bacterial cells and only the nucleic acid is introduced intracellularly by a complex mechanism. Animal cells do not have rigid cell walls and the whole virus can enter into them. Virus particles may be engulfed by a mechanism resembling phagocytosis, a process known as viropexis. Alternatively in case of the enveloped viruses, the viral envelope may fuse with the plasma membrane of the host cell and release the nucleopcapsid into the cytoplasm.

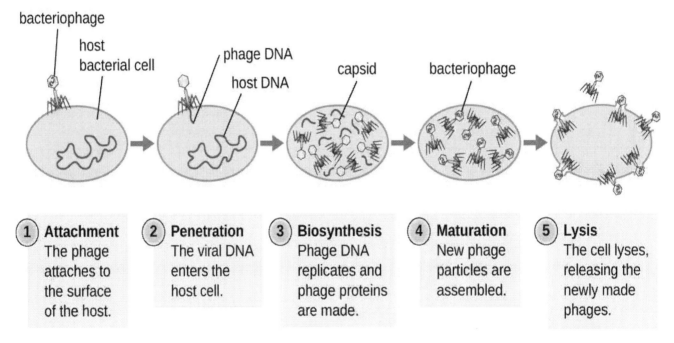

① Attachment	② Penetration	③ Biosynthesis	④ Maturation	⑤ Lysis
The phage attaches to the surface of the host.	The viral DNA enters the host cell.	Phage DNA replicates and phage proteins are made.	New phage particles are assembled.	The cell lyses, releasing the newly made phages.

Uncoating

This is an intermediate phase and in this process, the outerlayer is stripped and the nucleic acid is released into the cell. With most viruses, uncoating is effected by the action of lysosomal enzymes of the host cell. In the first step, lysosomal enzymes in the phagocytic vacuole remove outer coat. The inner core of the virus, containing the internal protein and nucleic acid, is released into the cytoplasm where the second step of uncoating is affected by a viral uncoating enzyme and the DNA is liberated.

Biosynthesis

This phase includes synthesis not merely of the viral nucleic acid and capsid protein but also of enzymes necessary in the various stages of viral synthesis, assembly and release. In addition certain regulator proteins also are synthesized which serve to shut down the normal cellular metabolism and direct the sequential production of viral components.

Biosynthesis consists of essentially the following steps:

a) Transcription of messenger RNA (mRNA) from the viral nucleic acid.

b) Translation of the mRNA into 'early proteins'. These proteins are enzymes which initiate and maintain synthesis of virus components. They may also include shutdown of host protein and nucleic acid synthesis.

c) Replication of viral nucleic acid.

d) Synthesis of "late or structural proteins", which are the components of the daughter virion capsid.

Maturation

Assembly of daughter virions follows the synthesis of viral nucleic acid and proteins. Virion assembly may take place in the host cell nucleus or cytoplasm. At this stage, the nonenveloped viruses are present intracellularly as fully developed virions, but in the case of enveloped viruses, only the nucleocapsid is complete. Envelopes are derived from the host cell membrane during the process of budding. The host cell membrane, which becomes the envelope, is modified by incorporation of virus specific antigens.

Release

In the case of bacterial viruses, the release of progeny virions takes place by the lysis of the infected bacterium. However in the case of animal viruses, release usually occurs without cell lysis, a process of budding from the cell membrane releases those viruses over a period of time. The host cell is unaffected and may even divide. The daughter cells continue to release virions. Progeny virions are released into the surrounding medium and may infect other cells. From the stage of penetration till the appearance of mature daughter virions, the virus cannot be demonstrated inside the host cell. This period during which the virus seems to disappear or goes 'underground' is known as the 'eclipse phase'. The time taken to release progeny virions after infection with virus is called the burst time. The number of progeny virus released after an infection is called burst size. A single infected cell may release a large number of progeny virions.

Lysogenic Cycle

Bacteriophages also replicate by the lysogenic method such bacteriophages are termed as temperate phages. Here the bacteriophage DNA get integrated to the bacterial chromosome during infection and forms an intermediate structure called prophage. This prophage can then undergo binary fission and thus the bacterial chromosome gets divided along with the viral DNA. The prophage can later undergo the same replicative cycle like the lytic cycle. This cycle is called the lysogenic cycle.

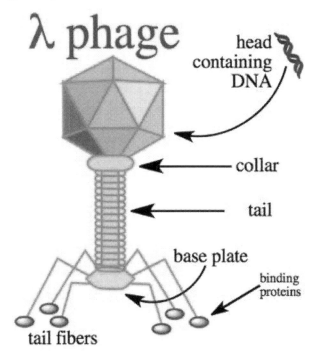

Table: Types of viruses

Types	Genome	Example
DNA virus	Double stranded DNA	Animal virus (Adeno virus, Papora virus, Pox virus, Herpes virus
		Plant virus (Cassava Mosaic virus, Cauliflower Mosaic virus, Dahlia Mosaic virus, Carnation Mosaic virus)
		Bacterial virus (Lambda phage, T phage)
	Single stranded DNA	Animal virus (Parvo virus)
		Plant virus (Maize Streak virus, Bean golden Mosaic virus, Beat early Top virus, Chlorosis striate Mosaic virus

RNA virus	Double stranded RNA	Bacteria virus (S13, M12, M13) Animal virus (Reo virus, Rota virus, Orbivirus, Blue Torgue virus Plant virus (Wound tumor virus, Rice dwarf virus, Maize rough dwarf virus)
	Single stranded RNA	Bacteria virus (ϕ 6) Animal virus (Picorna virus, Toga virus, Retro virus, Rhabdovirus Plant virus (Tobacco mosaic virus, Satellite necrosis virus, Wheat striate mosaic virus) Bacteria virus (MS2, F2)

Economic importance of viruses

Viruses have been primarily identified as pathogen, they are now found to have great economic importance. Due to the following characteristics, viruses are used for many beneficial uses.

a) Simple nature of genome

b) Host specificity

c) Capacity to direct host metabolism for the synthesis of their proteins and nucleic acids

d) Ability to be attached to the host genome

e) Ability to be isolated in pure forms

There are several uses of viruses like vaccine production, diagnosis, medicine and therapy, cancer prevention and control, biological warfare and in genetic engineering.

Use of virus in vaccine production

a) **Attenuated live virus vaccines**

These type of vaccines contain live viruses, whose virulence have been attenuated through different growth conditions. Most of the viral vaccines are attenuated and include the vaccine for measeles, mumps, yellow fever, rubella etc.

b) **Inactivated virus vaccines**

Such vaccines are produced by inactivation of viral infectivity by treatments with chemicals, heat, radiations or antibiotics. Purity and potency combined with adequate antigenicity are ensured during the inactivation process. The vaccine for cholera, rabies, polio, influenza, bubonic plague, hepatitis A, rabies etc are inactivated type.

c) **Synthetic peptides**

Viral nucleic acids can be readily sequenced and the aminoacid sequence of the gene products is predicted. Through genetic engineering techniques the nucleic acid can be designed to produce short peptides that correspond to antigenic determinants on a viral protein. The synthetic peptides do not change in the body. However it is observed that synthetic peptides is weaker than that induced by intact proteins.

d) Recombinant vaccinia virus as vaccines

Vaccinia virus has been used for production of vaccines. A number of genes coding for major antigens of pathogenic viruses have been inserted into vaccinia virus DNA and expressed in animal cell culture. Important viral antigens such as hepatitis B surface antigen, influenza virus hemagglutine proteins, rabies virus G protein and herpes simplex virus glycoproteins have been produced by such methods.

Use of viruses in diagnosis and research

a) Used as probes

Probes are oligonucleotides of short sequences (10-30 bases) of DNA or RNA which are used to detect the complementary sequences present in a sample. Diagnostic techniques like Southern blotting, northern blotting, dot blots, DNA and RNA sequencing, construction of genomic library etc. These short sequences of probes are generally obtained from viral genomes.

b) Production of enzymes

The enzyme reverse transcriptase produced by retrovirus has been extensively used in the generation of cDNA which is frequently used for research and clinical diagnosis. The enzyme ligase produced from T_4 phage virus is used in recombinant DNA technology as well as in cloning.

c) Bacteriophage typing

It is a technique of identifying the species of bacteria according to the type of virus that affects it. Such techniques are used in clinical samples analysis and research works.

d) Viruses as vectors

Lambda bacteriophages are extensively used in DNA cloning research. Different lambda vectors such as λ gt 10, λ gt 11etc are used as vectors in genetic engineering. M13 viral vectors are used to get single strands of cloned DNA which are used for DNA sequencing. Several modified vectors like M13-mp1, M13-mp8, M13-mp9 etc are produced from M13 genome.

Short notes

- Viruses, do not have a cellular organization. They contain only one type of nucleic acid, either DNA or RNA but never both.

- Viruses are obligate intracellular parasites. They lack the enzymes necessary for protein and nucleic acid synthesis and are dependent for replication on the synthetic machinery of host cells.

- The virion consists essentially of a nucleic acid core surrounded by a protein coat, called the capsid. The capsid with the enclosed nucleic acid is known as the nucleocapsid. The capsid is composed of a large number of capsomers. Viruses replicate by two methods: They are the lysogenic cycle and fytic cycle.

Fungi

Introduction

The fungi are a diverse group of eukaryotic microorganisms. The study of fungi is called mycology, and the individual who studies the fungi is a mycologist. For many decades fungi were classified as plants, but laboratory studies have revealed a set of properties that distinguish fungi from plants.

i) Fungi lack of chlorophyll, while plants have.

ii) The cell walls of fungal cells contain a carbohydrate called chitin not found in plant cell walls.

iii) Filamentous, fungi are not truly multicellular like plants, because the cytoplasm of one fungal cell mingles through pores with cytoplasm of adjacent cells.

iv) Fungi are heterotrophic eukaryotes, while plants are autotrophic eukaryotes.

For these above reasons fungi are placed in their own kingdom **Fungi**. These are saprobes with complex life cycles usually involving spore formation. A major subdivision of fungi, the molds, grow as long tangled strands of cells that give rise to visible colonies that resemble bacterial colonies.

Structure of fungi

With the notable exception of yeast, the fungi consists of masses of interwined filaments of cells called hyphae (sing, hypha). Each cell of the hypha is eukaryotic, with a distinct nucleus surrounded by a nuclear membrane and other eukaryotic organelles. The cell wall is composed of small amounts of cellulose and large amounts of chitin. Cellulose is a polysaccharide composed of glucose units linked together in such a way that most organisms cannot digest it. Chitin is a polymer of acetyl glucosamine units, i.e. glucose molecules containing amino and acetyl groups. Chitin gives the cell wall rigidity and strength, a function it also performs in the exoskeletons of arthropods. Fungal cells lack chlorophyll and photosynthesis is therefore impossible. Since they consume performed organic matter, fungi are described as heterotrophic organisms. Most are saprobic, except for parasite fungi, which cause diseases. Together with the bacteria, fungi decompose vast quantities of dead organic matter that would otherwise accumulate and make the earth uninhabitable. In many species of fungi the individual cells are separated by cross walls, or septa (sing. septum). The septa are not complete, however, and pores allow a mixing of adjacent cytoplasm. In other fungal species, the cells have no septa, and the cytoplasms and organelles of neighboring cells mingle freely. These fungi are said to be coenocytic. The common bread mold *Rhizopus stolonifer* is coenocytic, while the blue-green mold that produces penicillin, *Penicillium notatum*, has septa.

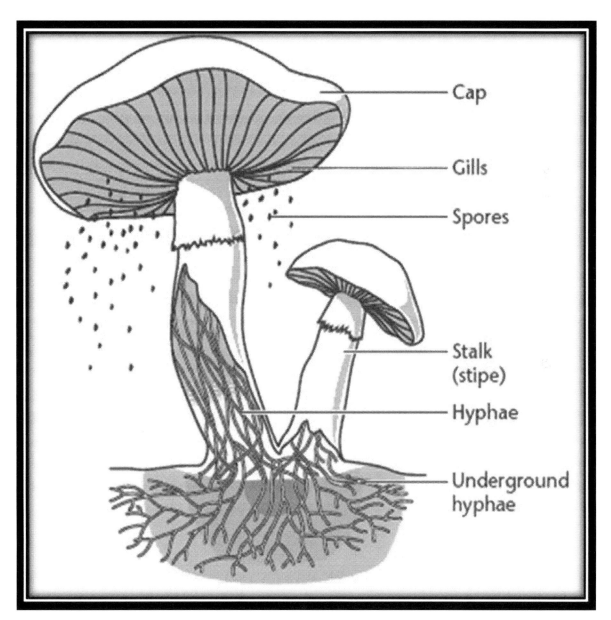

The hypha is the morphological unit of fungus and is seen only with the help of a microscope. Hyphae have a broad diversity of forms, and many are highly branched with reproductive structures called fruiting bodies. A thick mass of hyphae is called a mycelium. The mass is usually large enough to be seen with the unaided eye, and generally it has a rough, cottony texture.

Growth of Fungi

Many fungi live in a harmonious relationship with other plants in nature, a condition called mutalism. Other fungi called mycorrhizal fungi also live harmoniously with plants. The hyphae of these fungi invade the roots of plants. Mycorrhizal fungi consume some of the plants metabolic products. But plants are benefited by more efficient mineral uptake. Most fungi grow best at approximately 25° Celsius, a temperature close to normal room temperature. The notable exceptions are pathogenic fungi, which thrive at 37° Celsius. Usually these fungi also grow on nutrient media at 25° Celsius. Such fungi are described as biphasic (two phases) or dimorphic (two forms). Many have yeast like phase at 37° Celsius and a mold like phase at 25° Celsius. Certain fungi grow at still lower temperatures, such as at 5° Celsius found in the normal refrigerator. Many fungi thrive under acidic conditions at pH from 5 to 6. Fungi are aerobic organisms. Unicellular forms of fungi i.e., Yeasts multiply in the presence or absence of oxygen. Normally a high concentration of sugar is required for growth, and the laboratory media for fungi usually contain extra glucose in addition to an acidic environment. Example: Sabouraud's Dextrose Agar (SDA), Potato Dextrose Agar (PDA).

Reproduction in Fungi

Reproduction in fungi may take place by asexual as well as by a sexual process. The principal structure of asexual reproduction is the fruiting body. This structure usually contains thousands of spores, all resulting from the mitotic divisions of a single cell and all genetically identical. Each spore has the capability of germinating to produce a new hypha that will become a mycelium. Certain spores develop within a sac called a sporangium. These spores are called sporangiospores. Other spores develop on supportive structures called conidiophores. These spores are known as conidia (sing. conidium) from the Greek "conidios", meaning dust.

Some asexual modes of reproduction do not involve a fruiting body. For example, spores may form by fragmentation of the hypha. This process yields arthrospores. Another asexual process is called budding. Here the cell becomes swollen at one edge and a new cell called a blastospore, or bud develops from the parent cell and breaks free to live independently. Chlamydospores are thick walled spores formed along the margin of hypha, while conidia form from the tip of the hypha.

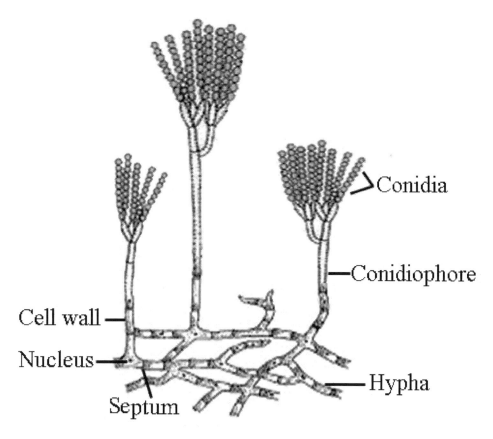

Figure: Penicillium: A mycelium bearing conidiophores

Many fungi also produce spores by sexual process of reproduction. In this process, the cells of opposite mating types of fungi come together and fuse. A fusion of nuclei follows and the mixing of chromosomes temporarily forms a double set of chromosomes, a condition called diploid. Eventually the chromosome number is halved and the cell returns to a condition where it has a single set of chromosomes, called as haploid condition.

Spores develop from cells in the haploid condition. Sexual reproduction is advantageous because it provides an opportunity for evolution of new genetic forms better adapted to the environment than the parent forms. For example, a fungus may become resistant to fungicides as a result of chromosomal changes during reproduction. Separate mycelia of the same fungus may be involved in sexual reproduction, or the process may take place between separate hyphae of the same mycelium. The process is essentially similar to that taking place in complex animals and plants.

The reproductive structures in the fungi are called **gametangium.** Male reproductive structures are called **anthredium** and the female reproductive structures are called **oogonium.**

Sexual reproduction in fungi is carried out in five different ways:

a) **Gametic copulation:** In this sexual method of reproduction, the fusion of gametes or sexual cells takes place.

b) **Gamete - Gametangial copulation:** in this method fusion occurs between the gamete of one sex with the gametangium of the other sex.

c) **Gametangial copulation:** In this method fusion occurs between the gametangia of the two sexes.

d) **Somatic copulation:** In this type of sexual reproductive cycle sexual fusion occurs between the vegetative cells.

e) **Spermitization:** In this method the spermatia unite with the receptive hyphae of the opposite strain.

Fungi produce different types of sexual and asexual spores. The spores, which are produced by asexual methods, are called asexual spores, which include blastospore, chlamydospores, sporangiospores, conidiospores and arthrospores while those which are produced by the sexual methods, are called sexual spores which include oospores, ascospores. basidiospores and zygospores.

Classification of Fungi

Variations in sexual process of reproduction provide important criteria for the classification of fungi. The true fungi belong to the division **Eumycota** in the kingdom Fungi. Other fungi in this kingdom are slime molds in the division **Myxomycota,** and the lichens in the division **Mycophycomycota.** Slime molds are complex organisms that have a motile stage and a fungus like spore producing stage. Lichens consist of a fungal mycelium containing a number of unicellular algae or cyanobacteria that perform photosynthesis. Members of the division Eumycota (true fungi) are divided into five classes based mainly on the type of sexual spore produced. They are: Oomycetes, Basidiomycetes, Zygomycetes, Deutromycetes and Ascomycetes.

The Yeasts

The word "yeast" refers to a large variety of unicellular fungi (as well as the single cell stage of any fungus). This group includes non-sporeforming yeasts of the class deuteromycetes, as well as certain yeast that form basidiospores or ascospores and thus belongs to the basidiomycetes or ascomycetes classes. The yeasts that are mainly considered here are the species of *Saccharomyces* used extensively in brewing, baking and as a food supplement. *Saccharomyces* is also called "sugar-fungus", due to the ability of the organism to ferment sugars. The most commonly used species of *Saccharomyces* are *Saccharomyces cerevisiae and Saccharomyces etlipsoideus,* the former is used for bread baking and alcohol production, the latter for alcohol production.

Yeast cells are about 8u.m long and about 5cm in diameter. They reproduce chiefly by budding, but a sexual cycle also exists in which cells fuse form an enlarged cell (an ascus) containing smaller cells (ascospores). The organism therefore belongs to the Ascomycetes group.

Short notes

- The fungi are a diverse group of eukaryotic microorganisms.
- Fungi are broadly classified into two groups based on their shape. They are unicellular forms called yeasts and multicellular forms called molds.
- They reproduce both by sexual and asexual methods. The fungi consist of masses of intertwined filaments of cells called hyphae.
- The cell wall is composed of small amounts of cellulose and large amounts of chitin.

Algae

Introduction

These are single cell eukaryotic organism having capable of photosynthesis. Certain **algae** are familiar to most people; for instance, seaweeds (such as kelp or phytoplankton), pond scum or the **algal** blooms in lakes. The study of this group is called as phycology.

Occurrence

These occur in great abundance in the ponds, streams, lakes, seas and in the oceans. Some of them are also found in damp soil, on rocks, stones and on other plants and animals. Some species of algae grow on the snow and ice of polar regions and mountain peaks, sometimes occurring in such abundance that the landscape becomes colored by the red pigments in their cells. At the other extreme, some algae grow in hot springs at temperatures as high as 55°C. Some algae have adapted their metabolism to the high salt concentration found in the salt lakes.

Characteristics of algae

 Algae have a wide range of sizes and shapes. Many species occur as single cells that may be spherical, rod-shaped, club-shaped, or spindle-shaped. Others are multicellular and appear in every conceivable form, shape, and degree of complexity, including membranous colonies, filaments grouped singly or in clusters with individual strands that may be branched or unbranched, and tubes (which may or may not be divided by cell walls). Some colonies are simply aggregations of single, "identical" cells that cling together after division; others are composed of different kinds of cells specializing in particular functions. These colonies become quite complex and superficially resemble higher plants in structure.

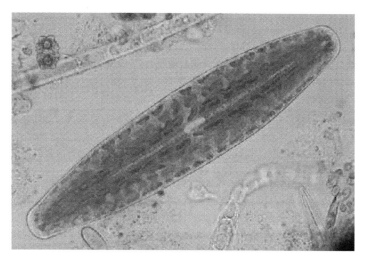

Figure: Microscopic structure of Algae

Algal cells are eucaryotic. In most species the cell wall is thin and rigid. Cell walls of diatoms are impregnated with silica, making them thick and very rigid: they are often delicately sculptured with intricate designs characteristic of the species or variety. The motile algae such ax Euglena have flexible cell membranes called periplasts. The cell walls of many algae are surrounded by flexible, gelatinous outer matrix secreted through the cell wall, reminiscent bacterial capsules. As the cells age, the outer matrix often becomes pigmented and stratified. Algae contain a discrete nucleus. Other inclusions are starch grains, oil droplets, and vacuoles. Chlorophyll and other pigments are found in membrane bound organelles known as chloroplasts. These chloroplasts may be massive structures situated near the wall (parietal) or embedded in the midst of the cytoplasm (asteroidal). They may occur as one, two, or many per cell: they may be ribbonlike, barlike, netlike, or in the form of discrete disks, as in green plants. Within the plastid (chloroplast) matrix or stroma are found flattened membranous vesicles called thylakoids. The fine structure of a eucaryotic algal cell is shown below.

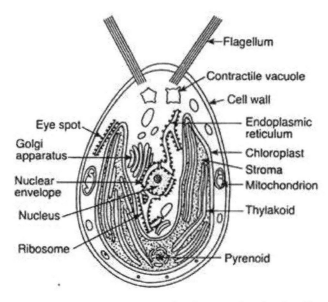

Figure: Fine structure of eukaryotic algal cell

Algal pigments

The chloroplasts of different divisions of algae containing similar pigments appear to have similar thylakoid arrangements. Chloroplast ultrastructure and pigment chemistry have been used as markers for algal phylogeny. It should be pointed out that several divisions of algae include colorless members, e.g.. certain species and genera in the *Euglenophycophyta*, the *Pyrrophycophyta*, and the *Chlorophycophyta*. These are sometimes considered protozoa. Nevertheless, some colorless flagellates have been shown to possess chloroplasts. There are three kinds of photosynthetic pigments in algae: chlorophylls, carotenoids, and biloproteins (also called phycobilins).

Chlorophylls

There are five chlorophylls: a, b, c. d, and e. Chlorophyll a is present in all algae, as it is in all photosynthetic organisms other than anoxygenic photosynthetic bacteria. Chlorophyll *b* is found in the *Euglenophycophyta* and *Chlorophycophyta* and in no other algal division. Chlorophyll *c* is more widespread and is present in members of *Xanthophycophyta*, **Bacillariophycophyta**, *Chrysophycophyta*, *Pyrrophycophyta*, *Cryptophycophyta*, and *Phaeophycophyta*. Chlorophyll d appears to be present only in the *Rhodophycophyta*. Chlorophyll *e* is rare and has been identified in only two genera of *Xanthophycophyta*, namely, *Triboneara* and the zoospores of *Vaucheria*.

Carotenoids

There are two kinds of carotenoids: carotenes and xanthophylls. Carotenes are linear, unsaturated hydrocarbons, and xanthophylls are oxygenated derivatives of these.

Biloproteins (Phycobilins)

These are water-soluble pigments, where as chlorophylls and carotenoids are lipid-soluble. Phycobilins are pigment-protein complexes and are present in only two algal divisions: the *Rhodophycophyta* and *Cryptophycophyta*. There are two kinds of phycobilins: phycocyanin and phycoerythrin. The proportion of one kind of pigment to another can vary considerably with changes in environmental conditions. Pigment quantitation is therefore not too reliable for use as a taxonomic feature.

Motility

The motile algae, also called the swimming algae, have flagella occurring singly. in pairs, or in clusters at the anterior or posterior ends of the cell. Since the advent of electron microscopy, considerable variation of taxonomic significance has been found in algal flagella. It will suffice for this discussion to mention three types: whiplash (cylindrical and smooth): tinsel (cylindrical and with hairlike appendages); and ribbon, or straplike. Some algae have no means of locomotion and are carried about by tides, waves, and currents. Others move about by means other than flagella. In some forms only the zoospores, the asexual reproductive cells, are motile. Some attach themselves to the substrate in the body of water where they are living and are occasionally broken loose by currents, which move them to new locations. A small red or orange body, the eyespot, is often present near the anterior end of motile algae. Other structures occurring in certain algae include spines or knobs on their exteriors and gelatinous stalks by which they may be anchored to some object.

Classification

 Although specialists do not agree on the details of algal classification, algae are generally classified on the basis of the following characteristics:

1. Nature and properties of pigments

2. Chemistry of reserve food products or assimilatory products of photosynthesis

3. Type and number, insertion (point of attachment), and morphology of flagella

4. Chemistry and physical features of cell walls

5. Morphological characteristics of cells and thalli

6. Life history, reproductive structures, and methods of reproduction.

Reproduction

Algae may reproduce either asexually or sexually. Some species are limited to one of these processes, but many have complicated life cycles employing both means of propagation. Asexual reproductive processes in algae include the purely vegetative type of cell division by which bacteria reproduce. A new algal colony or filament may even start from a fragment of an old multicellular type from which it has broken. However, most asexual reproduction in algae is more complex than this and involves the production of unicellular spores, many of which, especially in the aquatic forms, have flagella and are motile; these are called zoospores. The nonmotile spores, or aplanospores, are more likely to be formed by the terrestrial types of algae. However, some aplanospores can develop into zoospores.

All forms of sexual reproduction are found among the algae. In these processes there is a fusion (conjugation) of sex cells, called gametes, to form a union in which "blending of nuclear material occurs before new generations are formed. The union of gametes forms a zygote. If the gametes are "identical," i.e., If there is no visible sex differentiation, the fusion process is isogamous. If the two gametes are unlike, differing in size (male and female), the process is hetero gamous. As we proceed to the higher, though not necessarily larger, forms of algae, the sexual cells become more characteristically male and female. The ovum (female egg cell) is large and nonmotile, and the male gamete (sperm cell) is small and actively motile. This type of sexual process is termed oogamy. Exclusively male or exclusively female thalli also exist. Although these thalli may look alike, they are of opposite sex types, since one produces male gametes and the other ova. Such plants are called unisexual or dioecious. Plants in which gametes from the same individual can unite are said to be bisexual or monoecious.

The biological importance of algae

Most algae are aquatic organisms. Since 70 percent of the earth's surface is covered with water, it is probable that as much carbon is fixed (captured as carbon dioxide and changed to organic carbon compounds such as sugars) through photosynthesis by algae as in fixed by all land flora. As mentioned before, tiny floating algae constitute the phytoplankton of the sea and serve as an important food source for other organisms. These algae form the base or beginning of most aquatic food chains because of their photosynthetic activities and are therefore called primary producers of organic matter.

Algae are also present in soil even if their presence is not so obvious. They are probably important in stabilizing and improving the physical properties of soil by aggregating particles and adding organic matter. In addition, in many countries where the large red and brown seaweeds are plentiful, they are used as fertilizer.

Commercial products from algae

Many products of economic value are derived from algal cell walls. Three of these, agar, alginic acid, and carrageenan, are extracted from the walls of algae. Another, diatomaceous earth, is composed of millions upon millions of diatom glass walls deposited over time in either freshwater or the ocean. Agar and carrageenan are polymers of galactose, or galactose-containing compounds, with sulfate groups. Some of the sulfate groups are involved in the bonds between individual sugar residues. Agar and carrageenan are both called sulfated galactans, with carrageenan the more sulfated compound. Alginic acid consists of uronic acid residues. All three compounds are used either to make gels or to make solutions viscous. Carrageenan is extracted from the walls of several red algae. Species of Chondrus, Gigartina, and Eucheuma are most frequently used. Carrageenan has been used as a stabilizer or emulsifier in foods such as ice cream and other milk products. It is also used as a binder in toothpaste or in pharmaceutical products as well as an agent in ulcer therapy. Carrageenan is also useful as a finishing compound in the textile and paper industries, as a thickening agent in shaving creams and lotions, and in the soap industry: Agar is well known as a solidifying agent in the preparation of microbiological media. It is obtained from red algae. Species of Gelidium and Gracilaria are used extensively It is also important in the food industry where it is valuable in the manufacture of processed cheese, mayonnalse, puddings, jellies, baking products, and canned goods. In the pharmaceutical industry agar can be used as a carrier for a drug. Lotions and ointments can contain some agar. Alginic acid and its salts are obtained from the walls of brown algae, where they may represent as much as 25 percent of the dry weights. Species of brown algae producing this compound include Macrocystis, Agarum, Laminaria, Fu cus, and Ascophyllum. About 50 percent of the ice cream in the U.S. contains alginates, which provide a smooth consistency and eliminate Ice crystal formation. Alginates are also incorporated into cheeses and bakery products, especially frostings. Other industrial applications include paper manufacturing, the printing of fabrics, and paint thickening. An alginate material is used by dentists for making Impressions of the teeth for crowns, etc. The stipe (stemlike part) of the brown alga Laminaria japonica may be used by physicians for cervical dilatation and/or softening of the cervix (for example, in performing an abortion or placing a radium implant). The stipe is cut into sections, dried, and sterilized by ethylene oxide gas: such prepared stipes are available commercially. The section is put into place and swells gradually, rendering symmetrical dilatation of the cervical canal and softening of cervical tissue. Japanese physicians have used this method for more than a century. Diatomaceous earth is used primarily for filters or filter aids. It is especially suitable because it is not chemically reactive, is not readily compacted or compressed during use and is available in many grades The material is so finely divided that one gram of diatomaceous earth has 120 square meters of surface area, and yet in use up to 90 percent of the volume of the filter cake is open space. Diatomaceous earth is also used for polishing delicate surfaces because the diatom walls are so lightly silicified that they collapse under pressure and do not damage the surfaces.

Algae as food

Many species of algae (mostly red and brown algae) are used as food in the Far East. Of the red algae one of the most important is Porphyra: it is used as a food in Japan, where it is called "nori" and is usually processed into dried sheets. The algae are collected and washed in fresh water to remove debris, then chopped and spread on frames to dry into thin sheets. Nori is commonly toasted over a flame and sprinkled in soup or rice, or it is rolled around flavored rice with fish or vegetables to make a popular luncheon snack called sushi. Although several species are still collected wild, Porphyra has been cultivated since 1570. Today Japan's seaweed cultivation is the most advanced in the world. The nori industry is based mainly on *P. tenera* and *P. yezoensis*, although up to seven other species have been cultivated in Tokyo Bay in the past.

Other red algae, such as *Chondrus, Acanthopeltis, Nemalion,* and *Eucheuma* are locally collected and prepared Most of them are eaten as vegetables or in soups or prepared as sweetened jellies.

Red algae continue to be a significant food in China .Such algae have been a food staple and delicacy for the Chinese for thousands of years. For example, *Gracitaria* is mentioned in Chinese materia medica dating back to 600 B.C. In the past two decades, China has developed an impressive seaweed cultivation program. The species farmed are the edible brown alga L *japonica* as well as *Porphyra* and *Gracilaria*. *Porphyra* and other red seaweeds are expected to be increasingly important in the Chinese diet. In contrast to the diversity of species eaten by Asian and Polynesian peoples, red algal food usage in Europe and North America has centered around three genera: *Porphyra* or laver, Chondrus or Irish moss, and *Palmaria* or dulse. Laver is used extensively in the British Isles. The miners of southern Wales are the major laver consumers. About 40 to 50 tons of dried dulse are produced each year in Canada. The alga is collected in the Bay of Fundy and on the shores of Nova Scotia. Dulse is commonly eaten as a snack in taverns.

There is increasing interest in the use of the smaller forms of algae, especially *Chlorella*, as food for humans and domestic animals. When these organisms are grown under suitable conditions, they provide a rich source of protein comprising all the amino acids essential for animal growth. They are also a good source of carbohydrates and fats. The nutritive value of the microscopic algae has been demonstrated in tests with rats and chicks. Methods for mass cultivation of these plants, using waste products and sewage for their nutrition, have been developed. After algae have been grown on waste products, the residues can be disposed of in streams and lakes without causing pollution that would destroy aquatic animals. Although much can be said in favor of using algae in place of higher plants for human food, general acceptance of their use in this country is not to be expected until food from other sources is in short supply. In the meantime algae will doubtless find wide application as animal feeds or feed supplements.

Algae as pathogen

Although few algae are pathogenic, one, *Prototheca*, has been found to be a probable pathogen of humans. It has been found in systemic and subcutaneous infections, as well as in bursitis (an inflammation of the joints). *Prototheca* is a colorless *Chlorella*-like organism which superficially resembles yeasts. Several species are parasitic on higher plants; e.g. the green alga *Cephaleuros* attacks leaves of tea, coffee, pepper, and other tropical plants, causing considerable damage. Some algae live in the roots and fleshy parts of higher plants; liverworts, duckweeds, and other hosts to such algae do not seem to be harmed by their presence. Some of the extracellular inhibitors produced by algae have been shown by chemical analysis to be simple chemical substances; e.g., acrylic acid is produced by a unicellular alga in plankton. It is quite possible that as we learn more about algae and their extracellular secretions, their usefulness will become more apparent.

Some planktonic algae produce toxins which are lethal to fish and other animals. These toxins are extracellular, or they are liberated from the alga by bacterial decomposition of water blooms. It is known, however, that certain marine dinoflagellates belonging to the genera *Gymnodinium* and *Gonyaulox* cause death of aquatic animals by producing a high molecular weight neuro toxin. Those few dinoflagellate toxins which have been identified are among the strongest toxins known-50 times stronger than curare, a poison with which certain primitive peoples tipped their darts.

Shellfish poisoning occurs along the northeastern coast of North America as well as in the North Pacific. The organisms are *Gonyaulax catenella* on the west coast and *Gonyaulax excavata* on the east coast. Yearly outbreaks occur around Nova Scotia. The bloom of these dinoflagellates usually lasts just a few weeks, and often it is safe to eat shellfish about two weeks after the end of the bloom. The poisoning to humans comes from eating filter feeders, i.e, clams, scallops, or mussels, which filter the plankton from seawater as a source of food and accumulate the poison (toxin).

After ingesting sufficient toxin, the victim first experiences a numbing of the lips, tongue, and fingertips, usually within 30 min of eating shellfish. The diaphragm is soon affected and in serious cases respiratory failure can result.

Protozoa

Introduction

Protozoa (singular protozoan) derived from the Greek word "protos" and "zoon" meaning first animal. These are eukaryotic protists. They occur generally as single cells and may be distinguished from other eucaryotic protists by their ability to move at some stage of their life cycle and by their lack of cell walls Protozoa are predominantly microscopic in size. The majority are between 5 and 250 µm in diameter. Colonies of protozoa also occur. In a protozoan colony the individual cells are joined by cytoplasmic threads or are embedded in a common matrix. Thus colonies of protozoa are essentially aggregates of independent cells. The study of these eukaryotic protists is called protozoology. By a conservative estimate, there are more than 65,000 described species of protozoa distributed among seven named phyla. (In 1964 there were about 48,000 members of what was then known as a single phylum Protozoa) Slightly more than 50 percent of the species are fossil forms. Of the remaining 50 percent, some 22,000 are free-living species while 10,000 species are parasitic. Of the latter, only a few species cause disease in humans, but these few inflict much misery and death on millions of people. Even though the present species count appears staggering, there are hundreds of thousands of species yet to be described (even in 1983, an average of two new protozoan species were discovered daily).

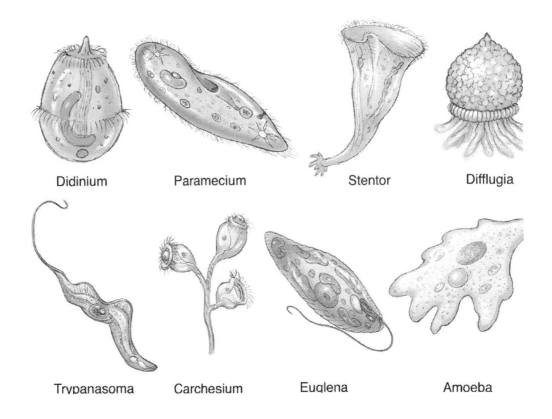

Didinium   Paramecium   Stentor   Difflugia

Trypanasoma   Carchesium   Euglena   Amoeba

Figure: Different species of protozoa

Occurrence of protozoa

Protozoa are found in all moist habitats. They are common in the sea, in soil and in freshwater. Free-living protozoa have even been found in the polar regions and at very high altitudes. Parasitic protozoa may be found in association with most animal groups. Many protozoa survive dry conditions by the formation of a resistant cyst or dormant stage. For example, the soil amoeba Naegleria is a resistant cyst in dry weather, is a naked amoeba in moist soil, and becomes flagellated when flooded with water. Parasitic protozoa can modify their morphology and physiology to cope with a change in host. For example, the malarial parasite Plasmodium produces male gametes in response to a drop in temperature on transfer from a warm-blooded mammalian host to a mosquito.

The distribution of trophic (vegetative) forms of protozoa in the sea and freshwater and of cyst forms in the atmosphere has resulted in the spread of free-living species throughout the world.

Ecology of protozoa

From the ecological standpoint, protozoa may be divided into free-living forms and those living on or in other organisms. The latter group is referred to as the symbiotic protozoa. Some of the symbiotic ones are parasitic and may cause disease. Others such as those found in the gut of the termite are beneficial to the host (live in a mutualistic association).

Light

Obviously, for those protozoa which bear chromatophores (these protozoa are considered algae by phycologists) and carry out photosynthesis, sunlight is essential. It follows also that those protozoa which feed on photosynthetic microorganisms also require sunlight, albeit indirectly. On the other hand. some protozoa avoid light and thrive in a environment where it is absent.

Hydrogen-Ion Concentration

Some protozoa can tolerate a wide range of pH, for example, pH 3.2 to 8.7. However, for the majority a pH range of 6.0 to 8.0 is optimal for maximum metabolic activity.

Nutrients

The protozoan population in an aquatic environment is influenced by the chemical constituents of the water. Some protozoa thrive in water rich in oxygen but low in organic matter (mountain springs, brooks, or ponds); others require water rich in minerals. Some grow in water where there is active oxidation and degradation of organic matter (the majority of freshwater protozoa, such as the ciliates). Still others prefer water with little oxygen but many decomposition products (e.g., black bottom slime and sewage). Some species have been found to live in both salt water and freshwater.

The nutrient supply in a habitat is a major determining factor in the distribution and number of protozoa within it. Species of Paramecium and other holozoic protozoa (protozoa that eat other organisms) must have a supply of bacteria or other protozoa (Fig. 19-1). As a general rule, holozoic protozoa which feed on a variety of organisms are widely distributed: those that are more selective and feed only a few species are limited in their distribution.

Temperature

Most protozoa have an optimum temperature of between 16 and 25°C: the maximum is between 36 and 40°C. The minimum temperature is less detrimental. The temperature tolerance varies with different environmental conditions. Even warm waters (30 to 56°C) of hot springs have been known to contain protozoa. The so-called red snow of high altitudes is due to the presence of several hematochrome-bearing flagellates (considered algae by some biologists). In the encysted stage (a thick-walled structure in an inactive stage), protozoa can withstand a far greater temperature variation than in the trophic stage.

Symbiotic Protozoa

The association between these protozoa and their hosts or other organisms can differ in various ways. The term symbiotic describes any type of coexistence between different organisms. In *commensalism* the host is neither injured nor benefited, but the commensal is benefited. Ectocommensalism is often represented by protozoa which attach themselves to a host's body. Endocommensalism is the association when the protozoan is inside the host's body, e.g., the protozoa which live in the lumen of the alimentary tract.

Mutualism occurs between some protozoa and their hosts. For example, certain flagellates are present in the gut of termites and digest the woody material eaten by the termite to a glycogenous substance which can be used by the host cells. If deprived of these flagellates, the termite dies; if the flagellates are removed from the termite gut, they too perish.
In parasitism, one organism-the parasite-lives at the expense of the other. The parasite feeds on the host cells or cell fragments by pseudopodia or cytostome (an opening for ingestion of food), or enters the host tissues and cells, living upon the cytoplasm and even the nuclei. As a result, the host may develop pathological conditions. The sporozoa are strictly parasitic and are among the most important of the disease-producing protozoa. Some parasitic protozoa parasitize other protozoan or metazoan whose bodies consist of many cells) parasites. Such an association is termed hyperparasitism.

Morphology of protozoa

The size and shape of these organisms show considerable variation. For example, Leishmania donovani, the cause of the human disease kalaazar, measures 1 to 4 μm in length. Amoeba proteus measures 600 μm or more. Certain common ciliates reach 2.000 μm, or 2 mm, and the tests (a kind of protective envelope) of some extinct (fossilized) members of Foraminiferida, the nummulites, measure up to 15 cm in diameter.

Intracellular structures

Like all eukaryotic cells, the protozoan cell also consists of cytoplasm, separated from the surrounding medium by a special cell envelop, and the nucleus or nuclei.

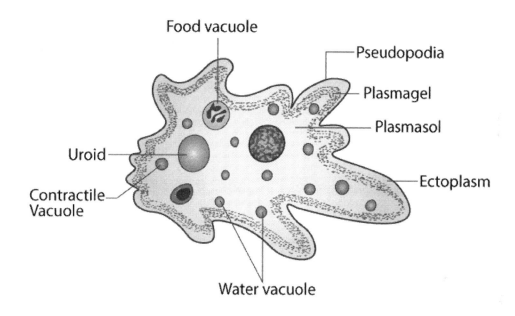

Figure: Microscopic structure of Amoeba

Cytoplasm

The cytoplasm is a more or less homogeneous substance consisting of globular protein molecules loosely linked together to form a three-dimensional molecular framework. Embedded within it are the various structures that give protozoan cells their characteristic appearance. Submicroscopic protein fibrils (fibrillar bundles, myonemes. and microtubules) are groups of parallel fibrils in the cytoplasm. Protozoan contractility is probably due to these fibrils. In several forms of protozoa, pigments are diffused throughout the cytoplasm. The hues are numerous; e.g., they can be green, brown, blue, purple, or rose.

In the majority of protozoa, the cytoplasm is differentiated into the ectoplasm and the endoplasm. The ectoplasm is more gel-like and the endoplasm is more voluminous and fluid,

106

but the change from one layer to another is gradual. Structures are predominantly found in the endoplasm.

Like other eukaryotic cells, protozoa have membrane systems in the cytoplasm. They form a more or less continuous network of canals and lacunae giving rise to the endoplasmic reticulum of the cell. Other structures in the cytoplasm include ribosomes, Golgi complexes or dictyosomes (piles of membranous sacs), mitochrondria, kinetosomes or blepharoplasts (intracytoplasmic basal bodies of cilia or flagella), food vacuoles, contractile vacuoles, and nuclei.

Nucleus

The protozoan cell has at least one eucaryotic nucleus. Many protozoa, however, have multiple nuclei (e.g., almost all ciliates) throughout the greater part of the life cycle. The protozoan nuclei are of various forms, sizes and structures. In several species, each individual organism has two similar nuclei. In the ciliates, two dissimilar nuclei, one large (macronucleus) and one small (micronucleus), are present. The macronucleus controls the metabolic activities and regeneration processes; the micronucleus is concerned with reproductive activity.

The essential structural elements of the nucleus are the chromosomes, the nucleolar substance, the nuclear membrane, and the karyoplasm (nucleoplasm). It has been shown that the number of chromosomes is constant for a particular species of protozoan. For example, Spirotrichonympha polygyra has 2 haploid chromosomes; Spirotrichosoma magnum has 60. Some protozoa divide only asexually (by mitosis). Others may divide either asexually or sexually (by meiosis).

Plasmalemma and other cell coverings

The cytoplasm with its various structures is separated from the external environment by a cell unit membrane (plasmalemma). The plasmalemma not only provides protection but also controls exchange of substances (semipermeable); it is the site of perception of chemical and mechanical stimuli as well as the establishment of contact with other cells (cell sensitivity to external factors). Although all protozoa possess a cell membrane, many protozoa have compound coverings of membranes modified for protection, support, and movement. Such combinations of membranes are referred to as a pellicle. In Euglena the pellicle is organized to ensure flexibility; in Paramecium it is quite rigid.

Actually, in its simplest form, the pellicle is the plasmalemma itself, e g. amoebas are surrounded by a plasmalemma only. However, even in these, some species (e.g. A proteus) have a diffuse layer of mucopolysaccharides over the plasmalemma. This layer is thought to play an important role in pinocytosis (uptake of fluids and soluble nutrients through small invaginations in the cell membrane that subsequently form intracellular vesicles) or in adhesion of the cell to the substratum.

The pellicle of a ciliate is thick and often variously ridged and sculptured. There may even be rows of elevated platelets and nodular thickenings. For example, the pellicle of *Paramecium* consists of three membranes, the outer one sculptured in a series of evenly distributed polygons. The contact between adjacent polygons results in a series of ridges, giving a latticed pattern.

Additional protective coverings external to the pellicle have also evolved for some protozoa. This results in the great diversity of forms exhibited by protozoa. These coverings are known variously as thecae, shells, tests, or loricae and occur in almost all major groups of protozoa. The thecae is a secreted layer directly apposed to the cell surface. Tests, shells, and lorica are coverings that are loose fitting. Special openings provide the connection with the environment. The coverings consist of very different materials. In general, they have an organic matrix reinforced by incrustation of inorganic substances such as calcium carbonate or silica.

We are familiar with mountain ranges or geological deposits of limestone, fusuline chalk, and green sandstone. These were formed by continuous sinking of calcareous shells and silicon skeletons of planktonic amoebas and other protozoa to the bottom of ancient oceans. For example, the white cliffs of Dover are made up of billions of scales of the phytoflagellates called coccolithopharids plus the shells of millions of foraminiferans.

Feeding structures

Food-gathering structures in the protozoa are diverse and range from the pseudopodia of amoebas through the tentacular feeding tubes of suctorians to the well-developed "mouths" of many ciliates. Amoebas gather food by means of pseudopodial engulfment. In ciliates the cytostome is the actual opening through which food is ingested. It ranges from a simple round opening to a slitlike structure surrounded by feeding membranelles. It is usually found anteriorly and remains open all the time in some groups; in other species it can be opened and closed.

An oral groove is an indentation in the pellicle of certain ciliates. It guides food toward the cytostome and acts as a concentrating device. The addition of membranelles to the oral groove makes it a peristome. On its edges are located cilia that function to facilitate feeding. The cytopharynx is a region through which nutrients must pass to be enclosed in a food vacuole.

Cysts

Many protozoa form resistant cysts at certain times of their life cycle. As indicated before, these cysts are able to survive adverse environmental conditions such as desiccation, low nutrient supply, and even anaerobiosis. In parasitic protozoa, the developmental stages are often transmitted from host to host within a cyst. Other kinds of cysts (e.g, reproductive) are also known.

Intestinal protozoa comprise about 50 percent of the parasitic species. In most instances they enter the alimentary tract as resting cysts, hatch in a suitable region, and then leave the host again as dormant cysts. By this means they can survive for long periods outside the host. Asexual reproduction in some ciliates and flagellates is associated with cyst formation. Sexual reproduction of sporozoa invariably results in a cyst.

The cyst wall is secreted as a closely fitting extracellular coat or structure. The cytoplasm is commonly attached to the cyst wall at one or several points: it is reduced in size and dormant.

Other protective structures

Some protozoa protect themselves with structures other than external coverings. These include various structures or materials formed within membrane-bound vesicles. For example, certain ciliates secrete a mucilage from sub pellicular vesicles called mucocysts. Several protozoa probably defend themselves by the expulsion of harpoon like trichocysts although their function has not been actually proved. Other protozoa, such as *Didinium* sp, have.

These have a threadlike tubular structure with an occlusion at the distal end which may contain toxin. When the toxicyst is discharged the toxin is distributed along the surface of the thread. Toxicysts are used to paralyze and capture prey, the toxin causes paralysis and cytolysis when it contacts protozoan prey.

In a similar manner haptocysts occur in the tentacles of suctorian protozoa and are used to contact and immobilize prey.

Locomotor organelles

Protozoa may move by three types of specialized organelles: pseudopodia. flagella, and cilia. In addition, a few protozoa without such organelles can carry out a gliding movement by body flexion.

Pseudopodia

A pseudopodium is a temporary projection of part of the cytoplasm of those protozoa which do not have a rigid pellicle. Pseudopodia are therefore characteristic of the amoebas (Sarcodina). These organelles are also used for capturing food substances.

Flagella and Cilia

The flagellum is an extremely fine filamentous extension of the cell. As a rule, the number of flagella present in an individual protozoan varies from one to eight; one or two is the most frequent number. A flagellum is composed of two parts: an elastic filament called an axoneme and the contractile cytoplasmic sheath that surrounds the axoneme.

In certain parasitic *Mastigophora*, such as *Trypanosoma*, there is a very delicate membrane that extends out from the side of the body with a flagellum bordering its outer margin. When the membrane vibrates, It shows a characteristic undulating movement; thus it is called the undulating membrane.

Cilia, in addition to their locomotor function, also aid in the ingestion of food and serve often as a tactile organelle. They are fine and short threadlike extensions from the cell. They may be uniform in length or may be of different lengths depending on their location. Generally, cilia are arranged in longitudinal, oblique, or spiral rows, inserted either on the ridges or in the furrows. Electron microscopy has shown that the fine structure of the flagella and cilia of all eukaryotes follows the same basic design. Sections show two central and nine double peripheral microtubules ("9 + 2" structure) along most of the length of the shaft, which is enveloped by a membrane continuous with the pellicle.

Reproduction of protozoa

As a general rule, protozoa multiply by asexual reproduction; the majority of higher animals reproduce by sexual means. This is not to say that sexual processes are absent in the protozoa. Indeed, many protozoa are able to carry out both asexual and sexual processes. Some parasitic forms may have an asexual phase in one host and a sexual phase in another host.

Asexual reproduction

Asexual reproduction occurs by simple cell division, which can be equal or unequal-- the daughter cells are of equal or unequal sizes, respectively. If two daughter cells are formed, then the process is called binary fission; if many daughter cells are formed, it is multiple fission. Budding is a variation of unequal cell division.

Binary Fission

The simplest form of binary fission is found in the amoebas. The pseudopodia are withdrawn before the nucleus divides. After the nucleus divides, the organism elongates and constricts in the center in order to form two daughter cells.

Amoebas with special protective coverings are more complex in their manner of binary fission, which is directly related to the type of covering they possess In those with soft coverings, the division plane is longitudinal along the body axis and the covering constricts into two halves. In those with more rigid coverings, part of the cytoplasm protrudes from the aperture (opening in covering) to secrete a new covering over its surface. Only after the formation of the new covering does nuclear division proceed, and binary fission is completed by cytoplasmic division.

In flagellates, with the exception of the dinoflagellates, fission is longitudinal along the major body axis. Since the flagella themselves are incapable of division, they must be regenerated from basal bodies (the blepharoplasts) which arise in the vicinity of the old basal bodies.

Thus multiplication of basal bodies usually precedes cell division. In dinoflagellates, division is at right angles to the cell axis because the flagella which determine the plane of division are not at the front end but at the side of the cell. Transverse fission is characteristic for ciliates. Fission occurs at a right angle to the long axis of the cell. In the simplest case of transverse fission, an equatorial furrow appears first which separates the surface cell layer into an anterior and a posterior half. A constriction follows leading to the separation of two daughter cells. Their form and structure usually indicate from which half of the mother cell they developed.

The presence of cilia and other complex organelles has a profound influence on cell division in the ciliates. For example ciliates have two types of nuclei---- the macronucleus, which determines vegetative processes, and the micronucleus, which is involved in sexual processes. During asexual binary fission the diploid micronucleus divides normally by mitotic division. The macronucleus undergoes DNA synthesis and divides into two portions without the regular reduplication of the chromosomes (amitosis). However each daughter macronucleus contains the full complement of genes (in fact. in multiple sets poly- ploidy). In some primitive ciliates found in marine sands of the intertidal zone the macronucleus is incapable of division: after fission of the organism a new one is formed from the micronucleus. In general, with regard to the other organelles, those originally present in each half are retained, and those which are lost during division are regenerated. Depending on the extent of differentiation of the species, divisions may involve extensive reorganizations, including transformation of preexisting structures and formation of new ones.

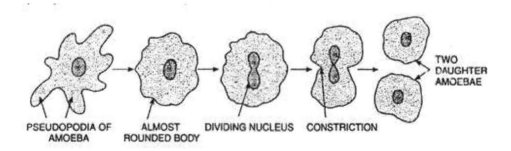

PSEUDOPODIA OF AMOEBA   ALMOST ROUNDED BODY   DIVIDING NUCLEUS   CONSTRICTION   TWO DAUGHTER AMOEBAE

Figure: Binary fission in Amoeba

Multiple fission

In multiple fission, a single mother (parental) cell divides to form many daughter (filial) cells. Division is usually preceded by formation of multiple nuclei within the mother cell, which then cleaves rapidly to form a corresponding number of daughter cells. Multiple fission is not as widespread as binary fission but it often takes place in addition to the latter process. In ciliates and flagellates, this type of fission is found in relatively few species. Multiple fission occurs commonly in the foraminifera, the radiolaria and the heliozoan. Perhaps the best-known examples of multiple fission are found in the sporozoa, e.g., in the malarial parasite Plasmodium where it is known as schizogony and serves to spread the parasite quickly in the host.

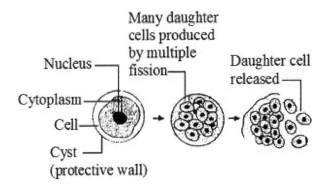

Figure: Multiple fission in protozoa

Budding

The term budding is not used in the same sense as mycologists use it in describing the asexual reproductive process in the yeast *Saccharomyces*. Instead, in protozoology it is often used to describe the varied processes by which sessile protozoa produce motile offspring. That is, the mother cell remains sessile and releases one or more swarming daughter cells. The swarmer differs from the parent cell not only in a lower degree of differentiation but also in the possession of special locomotor organelles. Some form of budding is found in all sessile ciliates and is used to disseminate the species while the mother cell remains in situ.

Budding can be exogenous or endogenous. The former involves formation and separation of the bud toward the outside. Definite exogenous budding is seen in suctorians when a portion or portions of an adult sessile suctorian bud from the parent, develop cilia, and swim away. In endogenous budding. which also occurs in many suctorian species, the swarmer is formed inside the mother cell.

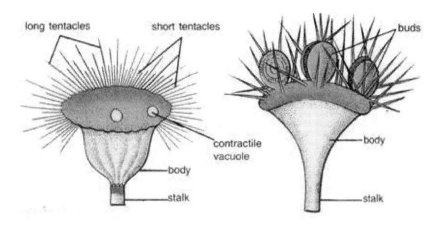

Figure: Budding in Protozoa

Sexual Reproduction

Various types of sexual reproduction have been observed among protozoa. Sexual fusion of two gametes (syngamy or gametogamy) occurs in various groups öf protozoa. Conjugation, which is generally a temporary union of two individuals for the purpose of exchanging nuclear material, is a sexual process found exclusively in the ciliates. After exchange of nuclei, the conjugants separate and each of them gives rise to its respective progeny by fission or budding. However, some ciliates show "total conjugation," with complete fusion of the two organisms.

When the gametes (which develop from trophozoites) are morphologically alike, they are called isogametes. When they are unlike in morphology (as well as physiology), they are anisogametes and can be either microgametes or macrogametes. That is, they are like the spermatozoa and the ova of metazoan, respectively. Thus microgametes are motile, relatively small, and usually numerous in comparison to macrogametes. Anisogametes are common among the sporozoa. For example, in *Plasmodium vivax* (a sporozoan that causes a type of malaria), anisogamy results in the formation of ookinetes or motile zygotes which give rise to a large number of sporozoites (long, slender bodies with an oval nucleus and firm cuticle, capable of producing new infection).

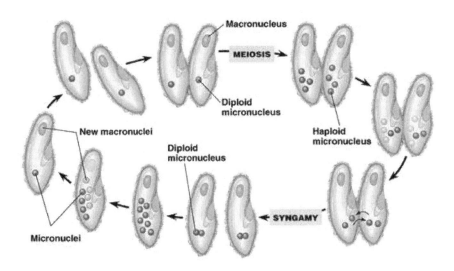

Figure: Sexual reproduction in Protozoa

The importance of protozoa

Protozoa serve as an important link in the food chain of communities in aquatic environments. For example, in marine waters, zooplankton (animallíke organisms) are protozoa that feed on the photosynthetic phytoplankton (plantlike organisms). They in turn become food for larger marine organisms. This food chain can be represented as follows:

Light energy ⟶ Phytoplankton ⟶ Zooplankton ⟶ Carnivores
           (Primary producers) (Primary consumers) (Secondary consumers)

Also of particular importance in the ecological balance of many communities, in wetlands as well as aquatic environments, are the saprophytic and bacteria feeding protozoa. They make use of the substances produced and organisms involved in the final decomposition stage of organic matter. This can be represented by the following sequence:

Dead bodies of producers and consumers, and their excretion products, including feces ⟶ Decomposition by fungi and bacteria ⟶ Ingestion of bacteria by protozoa.

It follows that microorganisms are important in the degradation of sewage. Although bacteria participate in a prominent way in the process, the role of protozoa is becoming more completely understood and appreciated. Biological sewage treatment involves both anaerobic digestion and/or aeration. Anaerobic protozoa such as species of *Metopus*, *Saprodinium*, and *Epalxis* are active in the anaerobic steps, while those treatment steps requiring aeration and

115

flocculation include the aerobic protozoa such as *Bodo, Paramecium, Aspidisca,* and *Vorticella.*

In the treatment of industrial wastes, where there is an accumulation of nitrates and phosphates, the settling tanks are illuminated to promote the growth of algae and protozoa. These protists remove the inorganic material from the water for their own synthesis. Water quality is improved, and the autotrophs are skimmed from the water surface, dried, and used as fertilizer.

Some protozoa cause disease in animals, including humans. They have caused untold misery. Such parasitic protozoa multiply within the host much as bacteria do. Some live only as obligate parasites and may produce chronic or acute diseases in humans. Some well-known protozoan diseases in humans are intestinal amoebiasis, African sleeping sickness, and malaria.

Protozoa have also become important research organisms for biologists and biochemists for the following reasons. Many protozoa are easily cultured and maintained in the laboratory. Their capacity to reproduce asexually enables clones to be established with the same genetic makeup.

Studies of mating types and killer particles in *Paramecium* have shown a relationship between genotype and the maintenance of cytoplasmic inclusions and endosymbionts. *Tetrahymena, Euplotes,* and *Paramecium* species have been used to study cell cycles and nucleic acid biosynthesis during cell division.

Nutrition and Metabolism of Microbes

Introduction

The term **Metabolism** is used to refer to the sum of all chemical reactions within a living organism. Chemical reactions either release or require energy; metabolism can be viewed as an energy-balancing act. Thus metabolism can be divided into two classes of chemical reactions: those that release energy and those that require energy. In living cells, the enzyme-regulated chemical reactions that release energy are generally the ones involved in **catabolism,** the breakdown of complex organic compounds into smaller ones. These reactions are called **catabolic or degradative, reactions.** Catabolic reactions are generally hydrolytic reactions (reactions that use water and in which chemical bonds are broken) and they are exergonic (produce more energy than they consume). An example of catabolism occurs when cells break down sugars into carbon dioxide and water.

The enzyme-regulated energy-requiring reactions are mostly involved in **anabolism,** the building of complex organic molecules from simpler ones. These reactions are called **anabolic, or faiosynthetic reactions.** Anabolic process often involves dehydration reactions (reactions that release water) and they are endergonic (consume more energy than they produce). Examples of anabolic processes are the formation of proteins from amino acids, and nucleotides and polysaccharides from simple sugars. These biosynthetic reactions generate the materials forced growth.

Catabolic reactions provide building blocks for anabolic reactions and furnish the energy needed to drive anabolic reactions. This coupling of energy requiring and energy releasing reactions is made possible through the molecule adenosine tri phosphate (ATP). ATP stores energy derived from catabolic reactions and releases it later to drive anabolic reactions and perform other cellular work. A molecule of ATP consists of an adenine, a ribose and three phosphate groups. When the terminal phosphate group is split from ATP, adenosine diphosphate (ADP) is formed, and energy is released to drive anabolic reactions.

ATP$\rightarrow$ ADP+ Pi +energy

Then, the energy from catabolic reactions is used to combine ADP and a Phosphate group to resynthesize ATP:

ADP+ Pi+ energy $\rightarrow$ ATP

Thus anabolic reactions are coupled to ATP breakdown, and catabolic reactions are coupled to ATP synthesis.

The role of ATP in coupling anabolic and catabolic reactions is important. Only part of the energy released in catabolism is actually available for cellular functions, as part of the energy is lost as heat. Because the cell must use energy to maintain life, it has a continuous need for new external sources of energy. The enzymes mediate the metabolic pathways of cell, which in turn is determined by the genetic makeup of the cell.

Energy Production

Nutrient molecules have energy associated with the electrons that form bonds between their atoms. When it is spread throughout the molecule, this energy is difficult for the cell to use. Various reactions in catabolic pathways concentrate the energy into the bonds of the ATP, which serves as the convenient energy carrier. ATP is referred to as having high-energy bonds, Thus the high-energy unstable bonds of ATP provides the cell with readily available energy for anabolic reactions.

There are two general aspects of energy production.

    a) The oxidation - reduction reactions

    b) The mechanism of ATP generation.

Oxidation-reduction reactions

Oxidation is the removal of electrons from an atom or molecule, a reaction that often produces energy, reduction means it has gained one or more electrons. Oxidation and reduction reactions are always **coupled,** i.e. each time a substance is oxidized, another is simultaneously reduced. The pairing of this reaction is called a **redox reaction or oxidation - reduction reaction.**

Most biological oxidation involve the loss of hydrogen **atoms,** they are also called **dehydrogenation reactions** in which, an organic molecule is oxidized by the loss of two hydrogen atoms, and a molecule of NAD+ is reduced. NAD+ assists enzymes by accepting the hydrogen atoms removed from the substrate. **One proton is left** over and is released into the surrounding medium. The reduced coenzyme, NADH, contains more energy than NAD+. This energy can be used to generate ATP in a later reaction.

In biological oxidation-reduction reactions, cells can use them in catabolism to extract energy from nutrient molecules. Cells take nutrients, some of which serves as energy sources, and degrade them from highly reduced compounds to highly oxidized compounds. When a cell oxidizes a molecule of glucose to CO_2 and H_2O, the energy in the glucose molecule is removed in a stepwise manner and ultimately trapped by ATP, which can serve as an energy source for energy requiring reactions. Compounds such as glucose that have many hydrogen atoms are highly reduced compounds, one containing large amount of potential energy. Thus glucose is a valuable nutrient for organisms.

The generation of ATP

Much of the energy released during oxidation-reduction reactions is trapped within the cell by the formation of ATP. A phosphate group is added to ADP with the input of energy to form ATP.

(Adenosine-P~P)+Energy+ (P) ➤ (Adenosine-P~P~P)

ADP--------------------------------------ATP

Figure: Generation of ATP from ADP

The symbol ~ designates a "high energy" bond. That is one that can readily be broken to release usable energy. The high-energy bond that attaches the third phosphate contains the energy stored in this reaction. When this phosphate is removed, usable energy is released. The addition of a phosphate to a chemical compound is called phosphorylation. Organisms use three mechanism of phosphorylation to generate ATP from ADP:

Substrate level phosphorylation

In substrate level phosphoryiation, ATP is usually generated when a high-energy phosphate is directly transferred from a phosphoryiated compound to ADP. Generally the phosphate has acquired its energy during an earlier reaction in which the substrate itself was oxidized.

Oxidative phosphorylation

In oxidative phosphorylation, electrons are transferred from organic compounds to one group of electron carriers. (Usually NAD+ and FAD). Then the electrons are passed through a series of different electron carriers to molecules of oxygen or other oxidized inorganic and organic molecules. This process occurs in the plasma membrane of prokaryotes and in the inner mitochondrial membrane of eukaryotes. The sequence of electron carriers used in oxidative

119

phosphorylation is called **electron transport chain**. The transfer of electrons from one electron carrier to the next releases energy, some of which is used to generate ATP from ADP through a process called **chemiosmosis.**

Photophosphorylation

The third mechanism of phosphorylation occurs only in photosynthetic cells, which contain light trapping pigments such as chlorophylls. In photosynthesis, organic molecules especially sugars are synthesized with the energy of light from poor building blocks such as carbon dioxide and water, Photophosphorylation starts this process by converting light energy to the chemical energy of ATP and NADPH, which in turn are used to synthesize organic molecules.

Metabolic pathways of energy production

Organisms release and store energy from organic molecules by a series of controlled reaction rather than in a single step. If the energy were released as a large amount of heat, it could not be readily used to drive chemical reactions and would infact damage the cell. To extract energy from organic compounds and store it in a chemical form organisms pass electrons from one compound to another through a series of oxidation-reduction reactions. A specific enzyme catalyzes almost every reaction in a metabolic pathway.

Carbohydrate catabolism

Most of the microorganisms oxidize carbohydrates as their primary source of cellular energy. During carbohydrate catabolism, the carbohydrate molecules are broken down to produce energy. Glucose is the most common carbohydrate energy source used.

To produce energy from glucose, microorganisms use two general processes; **cellular respiration** and **fermentation**. Both the processes usually start with the same step i.e. glycolysis, but later follow different subsequent pathways. The respiration of glucose typically occurs in three principal stages: **Glycolysis,** the **Krebs cycle**, and the **Electron transport chain. Glycolysis** is the oxidation of glucose to pyruvic acid with the production of some ATP and energy containing NADH.

The Krebs cycle is the oxidation of acetyl to carbondioxide, with the production of some ATP, energy containing NADH and another reducec electron carrier, $FADH_2$. In the **electron transport chain,** NADH and FADH, are oxidized, contributing the electrons they have

120

carried from the substrate to a cascade of oxidation-reduction reactions involving a series of additional electron carriers. Energy from these reactions is used to generate a considerable amount of ATP. In respiration, most of the ATP is generated in the third step.

Respiration involves a long series of oxidation-reduction reactions, the entire process can be thought of as involving a flow of electrons from the energy rich glucose molecule to the relatively energy poor CO_2 and H_2O molecules. The coupling of ATP production to this flow is by using energy from a flowing stream. The initial stage of fermentation is also glycolysis. Once glycolysis has taken place, the pyruvic acid is converted into one or more different products depending on the type of the cell. These products might include alcohol and lactic acid. There is no Krebs cycle or electron transports chain in fermentation. The ATP yield, which comes only from glycolysis, is much lower.

Glycolysis

Glycolysis is the oxidation of glucose to pyruvic acid. It is the first stage in carbohydrate catabolism. Most microorganisms use this pathway and it occurs in almost all living cells. Glycolysis is also called the **Embden-Meyerhof pathway.** The word glycolysis means splitting of sugar. The enzymes of glycolysis catalyze the splitting of glucose, a six-carbon sugar into two three-carbon sugars. These sugars are then oxidised releasing energy and their atoms are rearranged to form two molecules of pyruvic acid. During glycolysis NAD+ is reduced to NADH, and here is a nett production of two ATP molecules by substrate level phosphorylation.

Glycolysis does not require oxygen, it can occur in the presence as well as in the absence of oxygen. This pathway is a series of ten chemical reactions, each catalyzed by a different enzyme. Glycolysis consists of two basic stages, a preparatory stage and an energy conserving stage. In the preparatory stage, two molecules of ATP are used as a six carbon glucose molecule is phosphorylated, restructured, and split into two three carbon compounds Glyceraldehyde 3-phosphate and Dihydroxy Acetone Phosphate. (DHAP).

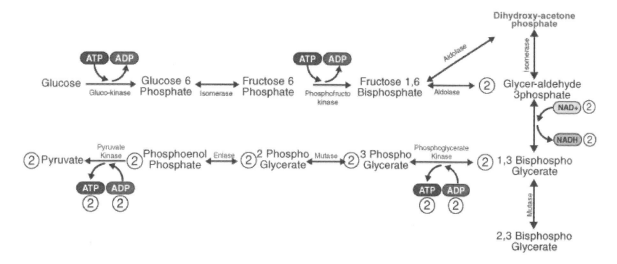

Figure: Glycolysis

The DHAP is then readily converted to Glyceraldehyde 3-phosphate (GP). The conversion of DHAP into GP means that from this point of glycolysis, two molecules of GP are fed into the remaining chemical reactions. In the energy conserving stage, the two-three carbon molecules are oxidized in several steps to two molecules of pyruvic acid. In these reactions, two molecules of NAD+ are reduced to NADH, and the four molecules of ATP are formed by substrate level phosphorylation. Two molecules of ATP were needed to start glycolysis and the process generates four molecules of ATP. So there is a nett gain of two molecules of ATP for each molecule of glucose that is oxidized.

Alternative to Glycolysis

Many bacteria have another pathway in addition to glycolysis for the oxidation of glucose. The most common alternative is the **Pentose phosphate pathway,** another alternative is the **Entner-Doudoroff pathway.**

Cellular Respiration

After glucose has been broken down to pyruvic acid, the pyruvic acid can be channeled into the next step of either fermentation, or cellular respiration. Cellular respiration, or simply respiration is defined as an ATP-generating process in which molecules are oxidized and the final electron acceptor is an inorganic molecule. An essential feature of respiration is the operation of an electron transport chain.

There are two types of respiration, depending on whether an organism is **aerobe,** which uses oxygen or an **anaerobe,** which does not use oxygen and may even be killed by it. In aerobic respiration, the final electron acceptor is O_2; in anaerobic respiration, the final electron is an organic molecule other than the molecular oxygen or, rarely, an in organic molecule.

Aerobic Respiration

The **Krebs cycle,** is also called the **Tricarboxylic acid (TCA) cycle or Citric acid cycle** is a series of biochemical reactions in which the large amount of potential chemical energy stored in acetyl CoA is released step by step. In this cycle, a series of oxidations and reductions transfer that potential energy in the form of electrons, to electron carrier coenzymes, chiefly NADH. The pyruvic acid derivatives are oxidized; the coenzymes are reduced.

Pyruvic acid, the product of glycotysis cannot enter the Krebs cycle directly. In a preparatory step, it must lose one molecule of CO_Z and become a two-carbon compound. This process is called **decarboxylation.** The two-carbon compound, called an acetyl group attaches to coenzyme A through a high energy bond, the resulting complex is known as **acetyl coenzyme A (acetyl Co A).**

During this reaction, pyruvic acid is also oxidized and NAD* is reduced to NADH. The oxidation of one glucose molecule produces two molecules of pyruvic acid, so for each, molecule of glucose, two moiecules of CO2 are released in this preparatory step, two molecules of NADH are produced, and two molecules of acetyl CoA are formed. Once the pyruvic acid has undergone decarboxylation and its derivative (the acetyl group) has attached to CoA, the resulting acetyl CoA is ready to enter the Krebs cycle.

As acetyl CoA enters the Krebs cycle, CoA detaches from the acetyi group. The two-carbon acetyl group combines with a four-carbon compound called oxaloacetic acid to form the six-carbon citric acid. This synthesis reaction requires energy, which is provided by the cleavage of the high-energy bond between the acetyl group and CoA. The formation of citric acid is thus the first step in the Krebs cycle.

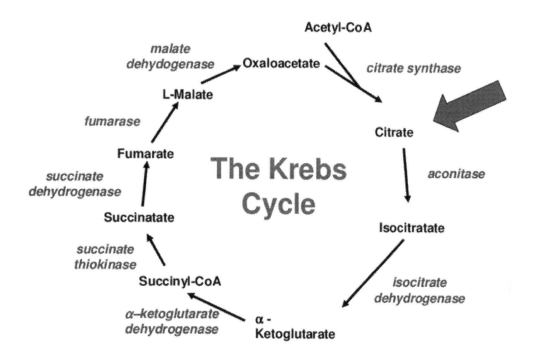

Figure: The Krebs cycle

The chemical reactions of the Krebs cycle fall into several general categories; one of these is decarboxylation. In step 3 isocitrate, a six-carbon compound is decarboxylated to the five-carbon compound called α-ketogutarate. Another decarboxylation takes place in step 4. Since one decarboxylation has taken place in the preparatory step and two in the Krebs cycle, Krebs cycle eventually releases all three-carbon atoms in pyruvate as CO_2. This represents the conversion to CO_2 of all six carbon atoms contained in the original glucose molecule.

Another general category of Krebs cycle chemical reactions is oxidation-reduction. In step 3, two hydrogen atoms are lost during the conversion of the six-carbon isocitrate to a five-carbon compound. In other words, the six carbon compound is oxidised. Hydrogen atoms are also released in the Krebs cycle in steps 4, 6 and 8 and are picked up by the coenzymes NAD+ and FAD. The NAD+ picks up two electrons but only one additional proton, its reduced form is represented as NADH, however FAD picks up two complete hydrogen atoms and is reduced to FADH2.

In Krebs cycle for every Iwo molecules of acetyl CoA that enters the cycle, four molecules of CO_2 are liberated by decarboxylation, six molecules of NADH and two molecules of FADH2 are produced by oxidation-reduction reactions, and two molecules of ATP are produced by substrate level phosphorylation. The CO_2 produced in the Krebs cycle is ultimately liberated into the atmosphere as a gaseous product of aerobic respiration. The reduced coenzyme NADH and FADH2 are the most important products of the Krebs cycle. Because they contain most of the energy originally stored in glucose during the next phase of respiration a series of reductions indirectly transfers the energy stored in the coenzymes to ATP.

The Electron Transport Chain

An electron transport system consists of a sequence of carrier molecules that are capable of oxidation and reduction. As electrons are passed through the chain, there is a stepwise release of energy which is used to drive the chemiosmotic generation of ATP. The final oxidation is irreversible. In eukaryotic cells the electron transport chain is carried out in the inner membrane of mitochondria, while in prokaryotic cell, it is found in the plasma membrane.

There are three classes of carrier molecules in electron transport chain. The first are called the flavoproteins. These proteins contain flavin, a coenzyme derived from the riboflavin, and are capable of performing alternating oxidation and reductions. One important flavin coenzyme is flavin mononucleotide (FMN). The second class of carrier molecules are called cytochromes, which are proteins that contain heme, an iron-containing group. The cytochromes involved in the electron transport chains include ctyochrome b, cytochrome c1, cytochrome c, cytochrome a, and cytochrome a3. The third class is known as ubiquinones or coenzyme Q. The electron transport chains of bacteria are diverse. Even a single bacterium may have several types of electron transport chain, but all of them achieve the same basic goal, that of releasing energy as electrons are transferred from high energy compounds to low energy compounds.

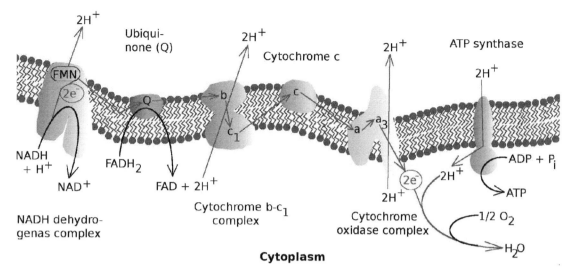

Figure: An electron transport chain system

The first step in the electron transport chain is the transfer of high-energy electrons from NADH to FMN, the first carrier in the chain. This transfer involves the passage of a hydrogen atom with two electrons to FMN, which then picks up an additional H^+ from the surrounding aqueous medium. As a result of the first transfer, NADH is oxidized to NAD* and FMN is reduced to $FMNH_2$. In the second step $FMNH_2$ passes $2H^+$ to the other side of the mitochondrial membrane, and passes two electrons to Q. as a result $FMNH_2$ is oxidized to FMN. Q also picks the additional $2H^+$ from the surrounding aqueous medium and releases it on the other side of the membrane.

The next part of the electron transport chain involves the cytochromes. Electrons are passed successively from Q to cytochrome b, cytochrome c, cytochrome c1, cytochrome a, and cytochrome a3. Each cytochrome in the chain is reduced as it picks up the electrons and is oxidised as it gives up electrons. The last cytochrome, cyt a3 passes its electron to molecular oxygen, which becomes negatively charged and then picks up the proton from the surrounding medium to form H_20. An important feature of the ETC is the presence of some carriers, such as FMN and Q, that accept and release protons as well as electrons, and other carriers such as cytochromes that transfers electrons only. Electron flow down the chain is accompanied at several points by the active transport of proteins from the inner side of the membrane to the outside of the membrane. The result is the building up of the protons on one side of the membrane.

The Chemiosmotic Mechanism of ATP Generation

The mechanism of ATP synthesis using the electron transport chain is called Chemiosmosis. Substances diffuse passively across membranes from areas of higher concentration to areas of low concentration. This diffusion requires energy, which is provided by ATP. In Chemiosmosis, the energy released when a substance moves along a gradient is used to synthesize ATP; the substance in this case refers to protons.

As energetic electrons from NADH pass down the electron transport chain, some of the carriers in the chain pump, actively transport the protons across the membrane. Such carrier molecules are called **proton pumps.** The phospholipid membrane establishes a proton concentration gradient, along with it there is an electrical charge gradient. The excess H^+ on one side of the membrane makes that side positively charged compared with the outside. The resulting electro chemical gradient has potential energy called the proton motive force.

The proton on the side of the membrane with the higher proton concentration can diffuse across the membrane only through special protein channels that contain an enzyme called **adenosine triphosphatase (ATP synthase).** When this flow occurs, the energy is released and is used by the enzyme to synthesize ATP from ADP and inorganic phosphate. Both prokaryotic and eukaryotic cells use the chemiosmotic mechanism to generate energy for ATP production. In prokaryotic cells the plasma membrane contains the electron transport carriers and ATP synthase. An electron transport chain also operates in photophosphorylation and is located in the thylakoid membrane of cyanobacteria.

Fermentation

Fermentation can be defined as the process that releases energy from sugars or other organic molecules, such as amino acids, organic acids, purines and pyrimidines. It does not require oxygen, it does not require use of the Krebs cycle or an electron transport chain, or the use of an organic molecule as the final electron acceptor. It produces only small amount of ATP molecules for each molecule of starting material, because much of the original energy in glucose remains in the chemical bonds of the organic end products such as lactic acid and ethanol.

During fermentation, electrons are transferred from reduced coenzymes to pyruvic acid and it derivatives, these final electron acceptors are reduced to the end products. An essential function of the second stage of fermentation to ensure a steady supply of NAD^+ and NADP+ so that glycolysis can continue. In fermentation ATP is generated only during glycolysis. Various microorganisms can ferment various substrates. The end products depend on the particular microorganism, the substrate and the enzymes that are present and are active.

Lactic acid fermentation

Glycolysis is the first phase of lactic acid fermentation. A molecule of glucose is oxidised to two molecules of pyruvic acid. The oxidation generates the energy that is used to form the two molecules of ATP. In the next step, the two molecules of pyruvic acid are reduced by two molecules of NADH to form two molecules of lactic acid. Thus the fermentation yields only a small amount of energy. Two important lactic acid producing bacteria are *Streptococci and Lactobacilli.* These microbes produce only lactic acid. Lactic acid fermentation can result in food spoilage. The process can also produce yogurt from milk and pickles from cucumber.

Alcohol fermentation

Alcohol fermentation also begins with the glycolysis of a molecule of glucose to yield two molecules of pyruvic acid and two molecules of ATP. In the next reaction, the two molecules of pyruvic acid are converted to two molecules of acetaldehyde and two molecules of CO_2. Two molecules of NADH to form two molecules of ethanol, next reduce the two molecules of acetaldehyde. Again alcohol fermentation is a low-energy yielding process because most of the energy contained in the initial glucose molecule remains in the ethanol, the end product.

Metabolic pathways of energy use

Up till now we have been considering energy production. Through the oxidation of organic molecules, organisms produce energy by aerobic respiration, anaerobic respiration and fermentation. Much of this energy is given off as heat. The complete metabolic oxidation of glucose to carbondioxide and water is considered a very efficient process, but about 45% of the energy glucose is lost as heat. Cells use the remaining energy, which is trapped in the bonds of ATP, in a variety of ways. Microbes use ATP to provide energy for the transport of substances across plasma membranes. Microbes also use some of (heir energy for flagellar motion. Most of the ATP however is used in the production of new cellular components. This production is a continuous process in cells, and in general is faster in prokaryotic cells than in eukaryotic cells.

Autotrophs build their own organic compounds by fixing carbondioxide in the Calvin-Benson cycle. This requires both energy and electrons. Heterotrophs by contrast must have a ready source of organic compounds for biosynthesis - the production of needed cellular components usually from simpler molecules. The cells use these compounds as both the carbon source and energy source.

The Integration of metabolism

We have seen thus far that metabolic process of microbes produce energy from light, inorganic compounds and organic compounds. Reactions also occur in which energy is used for biosynthesis. With such a variety of activity, you might imagine that anabolic and catabolic reactions occur independently of each other in space and time. Actually, anabolic and catabolic reactions are joined through a group of common intermediates. Both anabolic and catabolic reactions also share some metabolic pathways, such as Krebs cycle. For example, reactions in the Krebs cycle not only participate in the oxidation of glucose but also produce intermediates that can be converted to amino acids. Metabolic pathways that function in both anabolism and catabolism are called **Amphibolic** pathways, meaning that they are dual purpose.

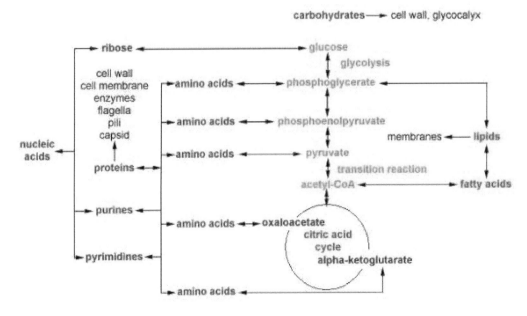

Figure: The integration of metabolism

129

Amphibolic pathways bridge the reactions that lead to the breakdown and synthesis of carbohydrates, lipids, proteins and nucleotides. Such pathways enable simultaneous reactions to occur in which the breakdown product formed in one reaction is used in another reaction to synthesize a different compound, and vice verse. Because various intermediates are common to both anabolic and catabolic reactions, mechanisms exist that regulate synthesis and breakdown pathways and allow these reactions to occur simultaneously. One such mechanism involves the use of different coenzymes for opposite pathways. For example, NAD' is involved in catabolic reactions, whereas $NADP^+$ is involved in anabolic reactions. Enzymes can also coordinate anabolic and catabolic reactions by accelerating in inhibiting the rates of biochemical reactions.

The energy stores of a cell can also affect the rates of biochemical reactions. For example, if ATP begins to accumulate, an enzyme shuts down glycolysis; this control helps to synchronize the rates of glycolysis and the Krebs cycle. Thus if citric acid consumption increases, either because of a demand for more ATP or because anabolic pathways are draining off intermediates of the citric acid cycle, glycolysis accelerates and meets the demand.

Nutrition of microbes

Microorganisms require nutrients for their growth and development. These nutrients include macronutrients and micronutrients.

The macro elements / major elements: are to be produced in large amounts. This includes carbon, nitrogen, hydrogen, oxygen, sulphur, phosphorous, potassium, calcium, magnesium and iron. There are many functions for these individual macronutrients. They are: Carbon, oxygen, hydrogen, nitrogen, sulphur and phosphorous are required for synthesis of components like carbohydrate, proteins, lipids and nucleic acids. Potassium is required for the activity of enzymes, especially in the protein synthesis. Calcium contributes to the heat resistance of bacterial spores. Magnesium is a co-factor for many enzymes, it complexes with ATP and also stabilizes the cell membrane and ribosomes. Ferrous and ferric iron play a part in cytochromes cofactor for enzymes and electron conjugating proteins. Major elements are required in milligram quantities. Nitrogen helps in the synthesis of purines, pyrimidines, carbohydrates, and lipids. Enzyme cofactors etc. Phototrops and non-phototrophic bacteria reduce nitrate to ammonia and incorporate the ammonia in association with nitrate reduction.

Trace elements/ Micro nutrients/ Microelements

It includes zinc, cobalt, molybdenum, nickel, copper and manganese. These elements form part of enzymes and cofactors. They also help in the catalysis of reactions and in maintaining the protein structure. Zinc is present in the active site of the enzymes. It is involved in the regulatory and catabolic sub unit in *Escherichia coli* aspartate carbamyl transferase. Manganese helps in the catalytic transfer of phosphate groups. Molybdenum helps in fixing nitrogen. Cobalt is an important component of vitamin B12. Trace elements are required in microgram quantities.

Metabolic diversity among organisms

Microbes are distinguished by their great metabolic diversity, however some can sustain themselves on inorganic substances by using pathways that are unavailable to either plants or animals. All organisms, including microbes can be classified metabolically according to their nutritional pattern of their source of energy and their source of carbon.

Based on the energy source, the organisms are classified as **Phototrops or Chemotrophs.** **Phototrops use** light as their primary energy source, whereas chemotrophs depend on oxidation-reduction reactions of inorganic or organic compounds for energy as (heir principal carbon source. Autotrophs are organisms, which can prepare food by themselves. Heterotrophs are those, which cannot prepare food on their own. If we combine the energy and carbon sources, we derive the following nutritional classifications for organisms: **photoautrophs, photoheterotrops, chemoautrophs and chemoheterotrophs.** Almost all of the medically important microorganisms are chemoheterotrophs. These infectious organisms catabolize substances obtained from the host.

Photoautrophs

Autotrophs can use CO_2 as their sole source of carbon. Some oxidize organic molecules to obtain energy. Many autotrophs are photosynthetic. **Photoautrophs** use light as a source of energy and carbondioxide as their chief source of carbon. They include photosynthetic bacteria (green and purple bacteria and Cyanobacteria), Algae, and green plants, the hydrogen atoms of water are used to reduce carbondioxide, and oxygen gas is given off. Because this photosynthetic process produces O_2, it is sometimes called **oxygenic.**

The chlorophylls used by these photosynthetic bacteria are called **bacteriochlorophylls,** and they absorb light at longer wavelengths than that absorbed by chlorophyll a.

Bacleriochlorophylls of green sulfur bacteria are found in vesicles called **chlorosomes (or Chlorobium vesicles)** underlying and attached to the plasma membrane. In the purple sulfur bacteria, the bacteriochlorophylls are located in invaginations of the plasma membrane (intracytoplasmic membranes). Several characteristics distinguish eukaryotic photosynthesis from prokaryotic photosynthesis.

Photoneterotrophs

Heterotrophs are organisms that use reduced form of organic molecules as the source of both carbon and energy. **Photoheterotrophs** use light as a source of energy but cannot convert carbondioxide to sugar; rather, they use organic compounds, such as alcohols, fatty acids, carbohydrates and other organic compounds, as sources of carbon. They are anoxygenic. The green nonsuifur bacteria such as *Chloftexus* and purple nonsulfur bacteria, such as *Rhodopseudomas* are photoheterotrophs.

Heterotrophs are further classified according to their source of organic molecules. **Saprophytes** live on dead organic matter and **parasites** derive organic matter from a living host. Most bacteria, and ail fungi, protozoa and animals are chemoheterotrophs. **Prototrophs** are microorganisms that require same nutrients as most of the naturally occurring members of its species. It get mutated, so cannot synthesize a molecule that can be converted to a nutrient. **Lrthotrophs** use reduced inorganic substances as the energy source.

Chemoautotrophs

Chemoautotrophs use the electrons from reduced inorganic compounds as a source of energy and use CO_2 as their principal source of carbon. Inorganic sources of energy for these organisms include hydrogen sulfide (H_2S) for *Beggiatoa;* elemental sulfur (S) for *Thiobacillus thioxidans;* ammonia (NH_3) for *Nitrosomonas;* nitrite ions (NO_2) for *Nitrobacter;* hydrogen gas (H_2) for *Hydrogenomonas;* ferrous ion (F_2^+) for *Thiobacillus ferroxidans;* and carbon monoxide (CO) for *Pseudomonas carboxydohydrogena*. **Organotrophs** extract energy or hydrogen from organic compounds.

Growth factors

Certain organic compounds are required because they are essential cell components or precursors of such components and cannot be synthesized by the organism. These are called growth factors. Three major classes are amino acids, purines and pyrimidines and vitamins.

Uptake of Nutrients by the Cell

There are different methods that are used for the uptake of nutrients by the cell. They are specific methods in which necessary substances pass through the selectively permeable membrane, which will not permit the free passage of many substances.

Different methods of uptake on nutrients include;

    a. Diffusion

    b. Active transport

    c. Group translocation

a. Diffusion

In this method molecules diffuse through the membrane. These are of two types:

> **Passive diffusion**

It is the process in which molecules move from a region of high concentration gradient to lower concentration due to thermal agitation. Rate of passive diffusion depends on size of concentration gradient between exterior and interior of the cell. So a large concentration is required for the uptake. Molecules of hydrogen, oxygen and carbon dioxide diffuse through this method of diffusion.

> **Facilitated diffusion**

The rate of diffusion increases across a selectively permeable membrane due to the presence of carrier proteins called **permeases,** which are embedded in the plasma membrane. It increases with the concentration gradient at low concentration of diffusing molecules. Carrier proteins resemble enzymes in their specificity for the substance to be transported and it transports only closely related solutes. No extra energy input is required. Concentration gradient decreases the inward movement of molecules.

b. Active transport

This method involves the transport of solute molecules to higher concentration or against concentration gradient with the input of metabolic energy. It involves carrier protein activity and it binds particularly with great specificity for the molecule to be transported. Similar solute particles compete for the molecules to be transported. It differs from facilitated diffusion in its use of metabolic energy and its ability to concentrate substances. Metabolic inhibitors that block energy production with inhibit active transport and will not affect facilitated diffusion. Bacteria use proton motive force to drive active transport. In **Antiport** the transported substances move in the opposite direction. **Simport** refers to the transport of two substances in the same direction.

c. Group translocation

In this method of transport molecules are transported into the cell, while being chemically altered. It transports variety of sugars into the cell and it is present in most prokaryotes, except *bacillus*. Aerobic bacteria lack the phospho transferase system.

Short notes

- The term metabolism is used to refer to the sum of all chemical reactions within a living organism. Metabolism can be divided into two classes of chemical reactions called anabolism and catabolism. In living cells, the enzyme-regulated chemical reactions release energy and there will be breakdown of complex organic compounds into smaller ones. These reactions are called catabolic or degradative, reactions. The enzyme-regulated energy-requiring reactions are mostly involved by the building of complex organic molecules from simpler ones. These reactions are called anabolic, or biosynthetic reactions.

- Various reactions in catabolic pathways concentrate the energy into the bonds of the ATP, which serves as the convenient energy carrier. ATP is referred to as having high-energy bonds. Thus the high-energy unstable bonds of ATP provides the cell with readily available energy for anabolic reactions.

- The sequence of electron carriers used in oxidative phosphorylation is called the electron transport chain.

- Photo phosphorylation occurs only in photosynthetic cells, which contain light trapping pigments such as chlorophylls.

- Glycolysis is the oxidation of glucose to pyruvic acid. It is the first stage in carbohydrate catabolism. Most microorganisms use this pathway and it occurs in almost all the living cells.

- There are two types of respiration, depending on whether an organism is aerobe, which uses oxygen or an anaerobe, which does not use oxygen and may even be killed by it. In aerobic respiration, the final electron acceptor is O_2; in anaerobic respiration, the final electron is an organic molecule other than the molecular oxygen or, rarely, an organic molecule. The electron transport chain regenerates NAD+ and FAD+, which can be used again in glycolysis and the Krebs cycle.

- The Krebs cycle, is also called the Tricarboxylic acid (TCA) cycle or Citric acid cycle, is a series of biochemical reactions in which the large amount of potential chemical energy stored in acetyl CoA is released step by step.

- The mechanism of ATP synthesis using the electron transport chain is called Chemiosmosis.

- Fermentation can be defined as the process that releases energy from sugars or other organic molecules, such as amino acids, organic acids, purines and pyrimidines.

- Microorganisms require nutrients for their growth and development. The nutrients include macro nutrients and micronutrients. Based on the energy source, the organisms are classified as phototrophs or chemotrophs.

- Autotrophs are organisms, which can prepare food by themselves.

- Heterotrophs are those, which cannot prepare food on their own.

Fermentation

Introduction

The industrial usage of microorganisms often requires that they be grown in large vessels containing considerable quantity of nutritive media. These vessels are commonly called fermentors and they provide the control and observation of many facets of microbial growth. Industrial fermentors are designed to provide the best possible growth and biosynthesis conditions for industrially important microbial cultures.

History and design of fermentors

De Becze and Liebmann (1944) used the first large-scale fermentor (above 20 litre capacity) for the production of yeast. But it was during the First World War; a British scientist named Chain Weizmann (1914-1918) developed a fermentor (or the production of acetone. The importance of aseptic conditions was recognized, so steps were taken to design and construct piping, joints and valves in which sterile conditions could be achieved and manufactured when required.

Basic functions of fermentors

The main function of a fermentor is to provide a controlled environment for growth of a microorganism, or a defined mixture of microorganisms, to obtain a desired product. Following criteria is used in designing and constructing a fermentor;

The vessel should be capable of being operated aseptically for a number of days and should be reliable for long-term operation. Adequate aeration and agitation should be provided to meet the metabolic requirements of the microbes. However, the mixing should not damage the microorganism. The power consumption should be low and temperature and pH control system should be provided. The evaporation losses from the fermentor should not be excessive. The vessel should be designed to require the minimal use of labour in operation, harvesting, cleansing and maintenance. It should have proper sampling facility. The cheapest and best material should be used and there should be adequate service provision.

Types of fermentors

Fermentors (bioreaclors) can be classified into two main types based on their shape, they are;

(i) **Tabular**

(ii) **Stirred tank.**

Cooling coils are provided to maintain constant temperature inside the bioreactor. It can be operated aseptically for many days and is simple in construction. The disadvantages are high power requirement, shearing on the organisms caused by vigorous agitation and inhibition exercised by the product.

Other types of fermentors include:

a) Fluidized bed bioreactor
b) Loop or air bioreactor
c) Membrane bioreactor
d) Pulsed column bioreactor
e) Bubble column bioreactor
f) Photo bioreactor
g) Packed tower bioreactor

Construction of fermentors

The criteria considered before selecting materials for construction of a fermentor are:

1. Sterilization should not cause any harm to the materials.
2. The material should be smooth with non-toxic and corrosion proof nature.

There are two types of such materials. They are stainless steel and glass, which are used in fermentors. Long and continuous use of stainless steel, sometimes show pitting. It is also important to consider the material used for aseptic seal. Sometimes it is made between glass and glass, glass and metal, joints between a vessel and detachable top or base plate.

Control of temperature

Since heat is produced by microbial activity and mechanical agitation, there is need to remove it. In certain processes using internal heating coil or jacket meant for water circulation, produces the extra heat.

Aeration and agitation

The main purpose of aeration and agitation is to provide oxygen required for the metabolism of microorganisms. The agitation should ensure a uniform suspension of microbial cells suspended in nutrient medium.

Design and operation

There are designs to provide the best possible growth and biosynthesis for industrially important cultures, and to allow the ease of manipulation for all operations associated with the use of fermentors. These vessels must be strong enough to resist the pressures of large volumes of agitating medium. The product should not corrode the material nor contribute toxicity to the growth medium.

In fermentation, provisions should be made to prevent contaminating microorganisms. Rapid incorporation of sterile air into the medium is required in such a way that the oxygen of air is dissolved in the medium and is readily available for microorganisms and carbondioxide produced by microbial metabolism is flushed out from the medium. Some stirring should be available for mixing the organisms throughout the medium so as to avail the nutrients and oxygen. The fermentor also contains an antifoaming agent, and a temperature control- The pH of the fermentation medium should also be checked. Other accessories consist of an additional inoculum tank or seed tank, in which the inoculum is produced and then added directly to the fermentor without employing extensive pipings which can magnify contamination problems.

The achievement and maintenance of aseptic conditions

It is necessary to sterilize and keep sterile the fermentor and its contents throughout the period of operations. The following operations may have to be performed to achieve and maintain aseptic conditions during fermentation:

a) Sterilization of the fermentor,

b) Sterilization of the air supply

c) Aeration and agitation

d) The addition of inoculum, nutrients and other supplements

e) Sampling

f) Foam control

g) Monitoring and control of various parameters.

Scale up of fermentations

The determination of the proper incubation conditions to be employed with large-scale production tanks as based on information obtained with various smaller sized tanks is called "scale up". This process allows to carry out laboratory procedure at an industrial scale. It is the best way to obtain fermentation information for production tanks directly in large tanks. However, this is not practical for (a) new fermentation (b) variation studies on a fermentation already in production and (c) valid experiments can't be carried out with only a single tank; one or more tanks are required as experimental contr6ls. Aside from these considerations, cost and media also affect the scale up.

Stock cultures

It is extremely important to maintain microorganisms for extended periods in viable condition, and in situations, which do not alter their desired product formation capacity. This condition is also true for strains used in biological assays. Thus, microbial species procured from various culture collection centers are maintained in viable conditions and are known as stock-culture collections. Stock cultures are of two types:

a) **Working stocks:** These stocks are used frequently and they must be maintained in vigorous and uncontaminated conditions on agar slants, agar stabs, spore preparations, or broth culture and are held under refrigeration. They must be checked constantly for possible changes in growth characteristics, nutrition, productive capacity and contamination.

b) **Primary stocks:** These cultures are held in reserve for practicals or new fermentation for comparative purposes, for biological assays, or for possible later screening programmes. These are not maintained in a state of physiological activity. Transfers from these cultures are made only when a new working stock culture is required, or when the primary stock culture is sub cultured to avoid death of the cells.

Culture preservation

Methods of preservations

A number of methods are used for maintaining organisms in a viable condition over a long period of time. Different microbes behave differently using a specific condition of growth. Therefore a method useful for one species may not be applicable to another. Some of the methods commonly used are as given below;

a) Agar slant culture

b) Agar slant culture covered with oil

c) Saline suspension

d) Preservation at very low temperature

e) Preservation by drying in vacuum

f) Lyophilization or freeze-drying.

Criteria used for the selection of microorganisms for fermentation

The selection of microorganisms used in fermentation processes and the methods used for the maintenance of these organisms are among the most important decisions that have to be made in designing an industrial fermentation process. The microbes should have the following attributes:

i) The strain must be genetically stable

ii) The strain should be readily maintained for reasonably long period of time,

iii) The strain must readily produce many vegetative cells, spores or other Structures.

iv) The strain should grow vigorously and rapidly after inoculation into inoculum vessel in the fermentation unit.

v) The strain should be a pure culture, free from other microorganisms including bacteriophages.

vi) The strains should be amenable to change by certain mutagens or a group of mutagenic agents.

vii) The strains should be able to protect themselves from contamination.

Methods of culture maintenance

There are three methods for culture maintenance which seem to be generally used in the fermentation industries:

a) Drying organisms on soil or some other solid,

b) Storing organisms on agar slants and

c) Removing the water from the cells or spores by lyophilization and storage of the dried product.

Production of microbial products

Alcohol production

Simple organic compounds act as feedstock for the chemical industry. Microbial production of one of the organic feed stocks from plant substances such as molasses is presently used for ethanol production. In modern era, attention has been paid to the production of ethanol for chemical and fuel purposes by microbial fermentation, by using sugar beet, potatoes, corn, cassava and sugar cane.

Both yeasts (Saccharomyces *cerevisiae, S.uvarum S. carlsbergensis, Candida brassicae, C.utils, Kiuyveromyces fragilis, K.lactis* and *Zymomonas mobilis* have been employed for ethanol production in industries. The commercial production is carried out with *Saccharomyces cerevisiae.* On the other hand, *S.uvarum* has also been used.

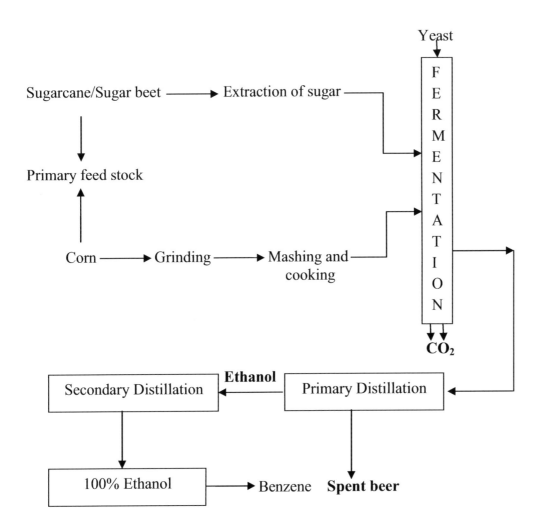

Figure: Ethanol production from molasses

Preparation of the medium

Three types of substrates are used for ethanol production.

a) Starch containing substrate

b) Juice from sugarcane, molasses or sugar beet

c) Waste products from wood or processed wood.

If yeast strains are to be used, then starch must be hydrolyzed, as yeasts don't produce amylases. If molasses are used for ethanol production, the bagasse can also give ethanol after fermentation.

Fermentation

Ethanol is produced by continuous fermentation. So large fermentors are used for the continuous production of ethanol. The fermentation conditions are almost similar, but the cultures and conditions used by each company are different. The fermentation is normally carried out for several days, but within 12 hours it will start production. After the fermentation is over, the cells are separated to get a biomass of yeast. The culture medium is processed for the recovery of ethanol. Ethanol is also produced by batch fermentation.

Recovery

Ethanol can be recovered up to 95% by successive distillation. To obtain 100 percent, it requires to form azetropic mixture of ethanol, water and benzene after distillation. In this process benzene - water - ethanol and then ethanol - benzene azetropic mixtures are removed so that absolute alcohol is obtained.

Production of wine

Wine is a product of grapes obtained after normal, alcoholic fermentation of yeast. Wine is basically the transformation of sugar of grapes by yeast under anaerobic conditions into ethanol, CO_2 and a small amount of by products. D- Glucoses and D- fructose are the two principal sugars of grape juice which yields ethanol and CO_2. Wine can also be produced by the fermentation of fruit juices, berries, honey etc.

Two kinds of grapes are used for wine production. The red grapes where the skin of the grape is red in color, which gives red wine. White grapes are used for the production of white wine. First the grapes should be stemmed, cleaned and crushed and then sodium or potassium meta bisulphate should be added to check the growth of undesirable organisms. The crushed grape is known as **must.** It is difficult to control the natural microbial population present in the must. So it is recommended to use a pure culture of wine yeast of proven quality.

The fermentation process

Adding 2-5 % of wine yeast, namely *Sacchafomyces cerevisiae* var. *eliipsoideus* in the must, carries out the process. The whole contents are mixed twice a day by punching the "cap" of floating grapes so as to allow the profuse growth of yeast due to increased aeration in the beginning. This process aids in the extraction of colour depending upon the quality of grapes used. Now the mixing should be stopped and anaerobic fermentation is allowed to progress. The temperature is maintained at 24° to 27°celsius for red wine for 3 - 5 days, and 10°ce!sius - 22°celsius for white wine for 7 to 21 days. The heat generated during fermentation may increase the temperature of the medium.

Recovery

The fermented juice is drawn off from the residue and stored under atmosphere of CO_2 for carrying out further fermentation, at about 21- 29° Celsius. If dry wine is to be obtained then the whole residual sugar should be fermented to yield ethanol.

The wine maybe pasteurized before ageing. During pasteurization, protein is precipitated and removed. It is cooled filtered and transferred to wooden tanks made up of white oak, red wood or plastic, concrete tanks for aging. Aging imparts flavor, aroma, sanctity and colour to the wine, after aging the wine is clarified, barreled and bottled. The final alcohol content of wine varies from 6 to 9 percent by weight or 8 to 13 percent by volume.

Kinds of Wine

On the basis of production of CO?, the wine produced is of two categories. They are:

a) **Still wine:** Those wines in which no CO_2 is produced during fermentation are called still wine's.

b) **Carbonated wine:** Those wines in which considerable quantity of -CO_2 is produced are called carbonated wine. On the basis of sugar content wines can be classified as **dry wines** (which have no unfermented sugar) and **sweet wines** (containing sugar). On distillation of wine, brandy is obtained. The alcohol percentage is increased up to about 2% in brandy. **Table wines** have a low alcohol content and devoid of sugar. Sherry is very popular in France and hence called French dry sherry. It is made from ripe and dried grapes with high sugar content.

Microbial production of citric acid

Citric acid is an organic acid sold in the market as an anhydrous crystalline chemical, or as crystalline monohydrate, or as crystalline sodium salt. Citric acid is used in soft drinks, jams, jellies, wines, candies, and frozen fruits. It is used in artificial flavors. In medical applications, it is used in blood transfusions as an effervescence product. In cosmetic industries, various astringent lotions have citric acid, where it is used to adjust pH and acts as a sequestrant in hair dressing and hair setting fluids. Since citric acid is a primary metabolite, it is produced during growth of the microorganism as a result of interruption of the TCA cycle. In this process good amount of sugar transport through the EMP pathway occurs which results in acetyl CoA production. In this case acetyl Co A condenses with oxaloacetic acid to yield citric acid.

Fermentation

Aspergillus niger has been the choice for the production of citric acid for several decades. A large number of other microorganism's such as *Pencilliun luteum, Citromyces, Aspergillus caivatus, Torulopsis* species, *Pichia* species, *Debaromyces daussenii* etc have been used for citric acid production. In industries, yeast is used rather than *A. niger because* of the possibility of using high initial sugar concentrations together with much faster fermentation.

In all the processes is of citric acid production, a variety of carbohydrates such as beet molasses, sucrose, commercial glucose, starch hydrolysate etc., are used in the fermentation medium. The starchy raw material is diluted to obtain 20 - 25% sugar concentration and mixed with a nitrogen source and other salts. Mainly three processes are carried out in fermentation. They are:

a) **Koji process:** It is a Japanese process in which special strains of *Aspergillus niger* are used with solid substrates such as sweet potato starch or wheat bran.

b) **Liquid surface culture process:** In this process aluminium or stainless steel shallow pans are used and the fermentation is carried out by blowing *aspergillus* spores over the surface of the solution for 5- 6 days, after which dry air is used. Spore germination occurs within 24 hours and white a mycelium grows over the surface of the solution. The initial sugar concentration will reduce after eight or ten days of inoculation. The liquid can be drained off and any portion of the mycelial mat left becomes submerged and activated. A small quantity of citric acid is produced during the growth phase. This is called primary metabolite. The mycelium can also be reused.

144

c) **Submerged culture process:** This process is quite economical. In this case the organism, *Japonicum saito* (a black aspergillus) is slowly bubbled in a steam of air through a culture solution of 15 cm depth. Since the organism shows subsurface growth and produces citric acid in the culture solution, the yields are inferior compared to the liquid surface culture fermentation. Aertion is required in the medium and anti-foam agents are also added to the medium. Continuous culture techniques are not considered suitable for use in citric acid production.

Recovery

The culture filtrate recovered is hazy due to the presence of residual antifoam agents, mycelia and oxalate. Ca $(OH)_2$ slurry is added to precipitate calcium citrate. After filtration the filtrate is transferred and is treated with H_2SO_4 which precipitate as $CaSO_4$. This is subjected to treatment with activated carbon. It is demineralized by successive passage through ion exchange beds and the purified solution is evaporated in a circulating granulator or in a circulating crystalizer. The crystals are removed by centrifugation and the remaining mother liquor is returned to the recovery stream Adding tri-n-butyl acetate, can also perform the solvent extraction. The solvent is then extracted with water at 70°C - 90°C. Citric acid is further concentrated, decolorized and crystallized.

Production of antibiotics

Antibiotics are chemical substances secreted by some microorganisms, which inhibit the growth and development of other microbes. Most of them are produced by *actinomycetes,* especially of the genus *streptomyces* and other filamentous fungi. The study of antibiotics began by the discovery of penicillin in 1929, when Alexander Flemming proved that the filtrate of a broth culture of *Pencillium notatum* has antibacterial properties in relation to Gram-positive bacteria.

Penicillin

Penicillin is an antibiotic, first produced from the fungus *Penciltium notatum.* Groups of several Penicillin differ from one another in the side chain attached to its amino group. Most of these penicillin are 6- amino penicillanic acid derivatives and all of them have the [3-lactum ring, which is responsible for antimicrobial activity. Penicillins act against Gram-positive bacteria and inhibit their cell wall synthesis. Penicillin producing species are required for the production of this antibiotic. The production medium contains ammonium sulphate, calcium carbonate, corn steep liquor, calcium hydroxide, glucose, sodium hydrogen phosphate and phenyl acetic acid. The pH is kept at 5.2 and the temperature for incubation is 23°C to 25° Celsius. Aeration and agitation are necessary.

Now a days Pencillins are produced commercially by *Pencillium chrysogenum,* a fungus that can be grown in stirred fermentors. The inoculum under aerobic condition can be produced, when there is glucose in sufficient amounts in the medium. If a particular pencillin (e.g. Penciliin G) is to be prepared, specific precursors are incorporated with the fermentation medium to get Pencillium G. Antifoam agents like vegetable oil is added to the medium before sterilization.

Steps involved:

Fermentation

The spore suspension is inoculated in flasks, each containing 15 grarr barley seeds. The flask containing 15-gram barley seeds is to be mixed with mother culture, and incubated at *25~* Celsius for 7 days. The spores which develop on barley seeds are suspended in distilled water to make a spore suspension. After testing the antibiotic activity, the flasks containing the seeds are ready for seeding in a fermentor. Three phases of growth can be differentiated during the cultivation of *Pencillium chrysogenum:*

a) First phase

In this phase the growth of the mycelium occurs and the yield of antibiotic is quite low Lactic acid present in corn steep liquor, is utilized at a maximum rate by the microorganisms. Lactose is used slowly. Ammonia is released into the medium resulting in the rise in pH.

b) Second phase

There is maximum synthesis of pencillins in this phase due to the rapid consumption of lactose and ammonia nitrogen. The myceliai mass increases.

c) Third phase

The concentration of the antibiotic decreases in the medium. The autolysins of the mycelium start liberation of ammonia and a slight rise in pH.

Recovery

When the fermentation cycle *(7 days)* is compleied the whole batch is harvested for recovery. Pencillin has the tendency that it remains in aqueous phase at normal pH and in solvent phase at acidic pH. This property of pencillin is used in the recovery of potassium pencillin from natural solutions. Once the fermentation is completed the broth is separated from fungal mycelium and processed by absorption, precipitation, and crystallization to yield a variety of semi-synthetic pencillins such as ampicilin, amoxycillin etc.

Streptomycin

It is effective against tuberculosis causing organism i.e. *Mycobacterium tuberculosis*. Prolonged use of streptomycin can result in neurotoxic effects and loss in hearing. *Streptomyces griesius* is used in the preparation of this particular antibiotic. The commercially available streptomycin is basically hyrochloride of streptomycin with calcium chloride. During the production of streptomycin, mannosidostreptomycin, or hydroxystreptomycin is also produced in the early fermentation. This salt is not economical and is easily converted to streptomycin by the action of *Streptomyces griesius*.

Media composition

Soya	:	10 g
Glucose	:	10 g
Peptone	:	5 g
Meat extract	:	5 g
Sodium chloride	:	5 g

The pH is kept at 6.5 – 7.0 and after inoculation the culture is incubated at 28^0Celsius.

Production

Streptomycin is produced by *Streptomyces griesius,* that is grown in stirred fermentors due to strong requirement of high aeration and agitation. The spores can be produced in medium, which provide enough sporulated growth to initiate liquid culture of mycelium. The optimum fermentation temperature is approximately 28°C and the whole process is completed within 5-7 days. There are three main steps for the production process of streptomycin:

a) First phase

Here growth of mycelium occurs. The proteolytic activity of *S. griesius* releases ammonia from the Soya bean meal, the carbon from Soya bean meal induces growth, but glucose is utilized at a minimum rate. The yield of streptomycin is low. There is a rise in the pH of the medium.

b) Second phase

The streptomycin is synthesized at a rapid rate in this phase, due to the rapid utilization of ammonia and glucose. The total incubation period lasts from 24 hours to 6-7 days. No mycelial growth occurs in this phase.

c) Third phase

The sugar depletes in the medium resulting in a depletion of cease of streptomycin production. The cells lyse, releasing ammonia resulting in a raised pH. Before lysis the fermentative material is harvested for recovery of streptomycin.

Recovery

After filtration the broth is treated with activated carbon and then efuted with dilute acid. The eluted streptomycin is then precipitated by solvent, filtered and dried before further purification.

Production of amino acids

Some amino acids are also produced by microbial fermentation. *Corynebacterium glvtamicum* and *Brevibacterium flavum* are involved in the synthesis of L-lysine and L-threonine from a common intermediate, aspartic acid.

L-Lysine production

Escherichia coti and Enterobacter are used for the production of this amino acid. The fermentation, media consists of glycerol. corn steep liquor and ammonium sulphate, in addition calcium carbonate is employed in the production medium. The pH is left neutral and incubation is carried out for 72 hrs at 28°C with high aeration. The yield of lysine is as high as 30 g / litre. Earlier this amino acid was produced by a two stage process using two different organism, the first stage was mediated by *Escherichia coli,* and the second stage was completed by *Enterobacter.* But now a single stage process using mutants of *Corynebacterium giutamicum and Brevibacterium flavum* are grown in synthetic medium containing glucose, an inorganic nitrogen source and a small concentration of either homoserine or methionine in addition to a small concentration of biotin.

Recovery

Lysine is a cell bound amino acid. But since the mutant strains are used for production it is secreted out and recovered.

L- Glutamic acid

It is produced by bacteria like *Micrococcus gtutamicus*. This organism is an auxotroph, but requires biotin in the medium for growth. The amino acid is present both intracellularly as well as leaked out in the medium subjected to optimum biotin level available for fermentation. Other Glutamic acid producing strains of microorganisms includes *Corynebacterium herculis. Arthrobacter globiformis, Brervibacterium divaricatum and Bacillus megaterium*.

Fermentation

The medium .contains glucose, ammonium acetate, potassium hydrogen phosphate, potassium sulphate, manganese sulphate, and an anti-foam agent. The fermentative organism used is *Brevibacterium divaricatum* (NRRL-B- 231). The incubation is carried out for 16 hours at 35^0C. At the beginning of fermentation 0.65 ml per liter of olive oil is added. The pH is set at 8.5 wilh ammonia and is automatically maintained at pH 7.8 during fermentation. Glucose feeding is done until the fermentations are completed.

Recovery

The Glutamic acid content is analyzed hourly. The fermentation is stopped after 30 - 35 hours with a yield of 100-g/ litre.

Production of enzymes:

Proteases

This group of enzyme catalyzes the hydrolysis of the protein molecule. The enzyme is a mixture of pectinases and proteases. These hydrolyze polypeptide fragments as aminoacids. Various bacteria such as *Bacillus, Pseudomonas, Closiridium, Proteus, Serratia* species and fungi namely *Aspergillus niger, Aspergillus oryzae and Aspergillus flavus are* the sources of proteolytic enzymes.

Production

A high yielding strain is selected and inoculated in special culture media containing 2 to 6 % of carbohydrate, protein and mineral salt. It is incubated for 3 days at about 37°C, with adequate aeration. The filterate is concentrated and the enzymes from culture are purified and absorbed onto some inert material such as saw dust. Many different media such as those containing wheat bran and soya cake are good for protease production.

Bacterial proteases help in digestion of fish liver to release oil. Such enzymes are also used in the beverage industry in clarification and maturing of malt beverages. On the other hand fungal proteases are active in the production of soya sauce and other continental food. They also remove the protein haze from beer and hydrolyze the gelatin protein material in fish waste.

Invertase (Saccharase or Sucrase)

This enzyme splits sucrose into glucose and fructose. It is widely distributed in nature. *Saccharomyces fragilis*, *Saccharomyces cerevisiae* and other *Saccharomyces* species are the richest source of enzyme Invertase. Invertase is produced in industries from bakers yeast.

Production

Industrially the enzyme Invertase is produced by special strains of yeast, which grow on bottom of the fermentation vessel. The medium contains sucrose, an ammonium salt, phosphate buffer and other materials. The pH is adjusted to 4.5. Fermentation is carried out for about 8 hours at 28°C to 30°C.

Recovery

The yeast cells are filtered off, compressed, plasmolysed and autolysed. The Invertase extracted may be dried or held in sucrose syrup. The enzyme can also be purified by dialysis.

Uses

Invertase is used in confectionary to make invert sugar for the preparation of ice creams, chocolate-coated candies. This enzyme imparts decrystallization of sugar syrups on standing. It is also used in the manufacture of artificial honey.

Production of Vitamins

Vitamin B12 (Cyanocobalamine)

Vitamin B12 is not a single compound but a group of closely related cobamides. These cobamides are also called pseudo B12 group. They consist of cobalt prophyrin nucleus to which ribose and phosphate are attached. Various cobamides differ in their purine, benzamidazole and other bases found in the nucleotide portion of the molecule. Vitamin B12 analogue having other' heterocyclic bases are either spontaneously produced by microorganisms or are produced by the addition of certain substances in the culture medium.

Fermentation

The nutritionally rich crude medium with glucose as a major carbon source is used in a two stage processes with added cobalt chloride. In the preliminary anaerobic phase (2-4 days), 5-deoxy adenosyl cobanamide is produced. In the second phase, which is aerobic (3-4 days) the biosynthesis of 5, 6-dimethyl benzamidazole takes place, so that 5-deoxy adenosyl cobalamine (B12) is produced. This compound is completely intracellular bound, which, after heat treatment is released in the solution.

If *Pseudomonas denitrificans* is used, it is a one stage process that occurs during the entire fermentation. Many other microorganisms can induce the formation of Vitamin B12. Eg.: *Bacillus megaterium, Propionibacterium ruber, Micromonospora species. Klebsiella pneumoniae, etc.* The Human intestinal microorganisms also produce Vitamin B12. Humans obtain vitamin B12 mainly from food.

Riboflavin

Riboflavin is also called lactoflavin. It contains the prosthetic group FMN -(Flavin Mononucleotide) or FAD- (Flavin Adenine nucleotide). Several microorganisms like *Clostridium acetobutylyticum, Mycobacterium smegmatitis, Candida flareri, Erymothedum ashbyii and Ashbya gossypi are* used for the commercial production of Riboflavin. It is also produced by chemical synthesis, but biotransformation of Glucose to D-ribose by mutants of *Bacillus pumulis* and subsequent chemical conversion to riboflavin accounts for 50% of the worldwide production. Riboflavin is an alloxazine derivative, which consists of a pyridine ring condensed to a benzene ring. The side chain consists of C5- poly hydroxy group.

Production

The production medium contains corn steep liquor, commercial peptone, and soybean oil, along with peptones, glycine, or yeast extract. The glucose and inositol increases the riboflavin production. The medium is kept at $2G^3C$ - $28^=C$ for 4 - days incubation time after inoculation of submerged growth of *Ashbya gossypi*. Excess air inhibits the growth of this particular fungus i.e. the mycelium production is inhibited.

The fermentation progresses in three stages, they are:

a) **First phase:** In this phase rapid growth occurs with small quantity of riboflavin production. The utilization of glucose occurs resulting in a decrease in pH due to accumulation of pyruvate. By the end of this phase glucose is exhausted and the growth ceases.

b) **Second phase:** In this phase sporulation occurs. The pyruvate decreases in concentration. Ammonia accumulates because of an increase in deaminase activity. The pH reaches towards alkalinity.

c) **Third phase:** In this phase there is rapid synthesis of cell bound riboflavin (FNM and FAD). This phase is accompanied by a rapid increase in catalase activity and subsequently the cytochromes disappear. As the fermentation completes autolysis takes place, which releases free riboflavin into the medium. It is observed that certain purines stimulate riboflavin production without simultaneous growth stimulation.

The riboflavin is present both in solution and bound to the mycelium in the fermentation broth. The bound vitamin is released from the cells by heat treatment and the mycelium is separated and discarded. The riboflavin is then further purified. Crystalline riboflavin preparations of high purity have been produced using *Saccharomyces cerevisiae* with acetate as the sole source of carbon.

Uses of Riboflavin:

It is essential for growth and reproduction. It is also recommend as a feed additive in animal nutrition. Riboflavin deficiency in rats causes stunted growth, dermatitis, and eye damage. Ariboflavinosis is a disease in humans caused by riboflavin deficiency.

Short notes

- Fermentors are used to provide a controlled environment for growth of a particular microorganism, or a defined mixture of microorganisms. The fermentor should be capable of being operated aseptically for a number of days and should be reliable for long-term operation. Adequate aeration and agitation should be provided to meet the metabolic requirements of the microbes; the mixing should not damage the microorganism.

- Fermentors (bioreactors) can be classified into two main types based on their shape, they are: Tabular tank and Stirred tank reactors. Other types include Fluidized bed bioreactor, Air bioreactor Membrane bioreactor, Pulsed column bioreactor, Bubble column bioreactor, Photo bioreactor and Packed tower bioreactor.

- It is necessary to sterilize and keep sterile fermentor and its contents throughout the fermentation process.

- Microbial production of ethanol is done from plant substances such as molasses. The commercial production is carried out with *Saccharomyces cerevisiae,* using sugar beet, potatoes, corn, cassava and sugarcane.

- Wine is a product of grapes obtained after normal, alcoholic fermentation by yeast.

- Citric acid is an organic acid sold in the market as an anhydrous crystalline chemical, or as crystalline monohydrate, or as crystalline sodium salt. *Aspergillus niger* has been the organism of choice for the production of citric acid for several decades by methods like Liquid surface culture process, Koji process, and Submerged culture process.

- Antibiotics are chemical substances secreted by some microorganisms, which inhibit the growth and development of other microbes. Pencillins are produced commercially by *Pencillium chrysogenum,* a fungus that can be grown in stirred fermentors. *Streptomyces griesius* is used in the preparation of Streptomycin.

- Amino acids are also produced by microbial fermentation. *Corynebacterium glutamicum* and *Brevibacterium flavum* are involved in the synthesis of L- lysine and L- threonine from a common intermediate, aspartic acid.

- *Pseudomonas denitrificans* is used for the production of Vitamin B12, which is a one stage process. Many other microorganisms can also induce the formation of Vitamin B12.

Printed in Great Britain
by Amazon